Still Going Strong

Paul & Joan -

great to meet
you - Keep on adventuring -

Cheers John

Still Going Strong

BACKPACKING ADVENTURES
THROUGH MY 60'S

Talie Morrison
Adventurer, Backpacker, and Grandmother

ISBN: 0692776400
ISBN 13: 9780692776407
Library of Congress Control Number: 2016914643
Natalie Morrison, Crested Butte, CO

Table of Contents

Introduction

• • •

WHAT ON EARTH AM I DOING HERE?

WELCOME TO JANUARY, 2006. I wish I could bid you a warmer welcome. But where I am right now, it is bitterly cold.

My name is Natalie Morrison. But please, call me Talie. I am a 60 year old American woman, camping alone in a remote mountain pass on the South Island of New Zealand. It is a three-day walk to the nearest road. It's 5:00am, and I am blind to my surroundings in the darkness. The wind is howling, and the rain is pouring. Water seeps into my down sleeping bag. My feet are now getting wet. My tarp is useless and flaps noisily in the wind. I am cold and drenched to the bone. It feels like some mischievous kid is throwing buckets of icy water on me.

I untangle myself from my flimsy, sodden tarp and wiggle out of my soggy sleeping bag. As I stand up, the wind knocks me flat.

WHAM!

I try to stand up again...

WHAM!

I crawl behind some rocks for a little bit of shelter, and try to tame my rain gear enough to cover myself. I need to get out of this vicious wind and rain, and down into the relative calm of the river valley, but I can't do anything until it gets light.

When it is light enough, all I can see is more rain. Sheets of rain, going in all directions in this wild wind. How on earth do I get out of here? Climbing up and over the high mountain pass is not an option in this storm. Too treacherous. Too dangerous. Too many ways I can hurt myself. Badly.

I think about returning to the hut where I started this leg of my journey. That's not an option either, as it would mean going back over a pass which is now invisible under a shroud of thick cloud. I consult my map, which flaps madly in the wind. It sounds like a famous breakfast cereal – Snap, Crackle and Pop! - but nowhere near as much fun. Once I finally manage to bring the map under some sort of control, I see another route which will take me down to the river valley.

Things are looking up!

I put all my wet gear into my pack and hoist it onto my back. With what feels like a sack of cement on my back, I start to descend towards the river. All that steep climbing I did yesterday is now steep and slippery downward scrambling. I slip and slide on the wet grass, and spend as much time on my backside as I do on my feet. Finally I get off the slippery slopes and arrive in the valley.

Things aren't much better down here, to be honest with you. I am stranded in a spot where two creeks come together. Because of the storm, these two gentle creeks are now raging torrents. It is a well-known fact in the New Zealand backcountry, or anywhere for that matter, that crossing swollen creeks is a very dangerous thing to do. So here I am, stuck between two creeks, and neither of them is crossable. It looks like I'll have to wait until the water goes down. The rain is still bucketing down. This could be a long wait...

By this time it is noon, but there is no midday sun to warm me. I rig up my tarp again, and try to start a small fire. But everything is so damp, including the air, that I can only get things to smolder. I am getting even colder, and I desperately need some energy burning in my body to warm me up. I crank up my cook stove and make a cup of tea. This warms me a little, but as I don't know how long I might be stuck here, and I don't want to use all my fuel at once, regular cups of tea are off the menu. So I try walking around the area where I am stuck. This doesn't work. I'm only getting wetter from the bushes, instead of getting warmer.

"Ok," I think, "Hypothermia is a potential problem here. A potentially big problem. A potentially fatal problem".

With this cheering thought in my head, I ponder other ways to get warm. A good idea is to use the big muscles of my legs, and get the quads working for me by walking uphill. But I'm in the flats of the river valley, and there aren't any big hills. Then, from somewhere out of the mist, an idea floats into my brain. I haul a couple of big rocks from the edge of the river, and build myself a step. I'll do step aerobics!

Eureka!

With my heavy pack on my back, I do step aerobics for about 30 minutes. When I am close to sweating, I relax for 45 minutes. When I get cold again, back to step aerobics. I spend a couple of hours stepping on and off a rock in the river valley, all the while pretending I am at the gym doing my best Richard Simmons.

I keep my eyes on the water levels in the two creeks. I use a boulder in the middle of one creek as a guide. Slowly but surely, the boulder becomes less covered with water. It is only drizzling now, and the water level is coming down a little. Finally, at about 8:00 pm (Have I really been in this spot for eight hours??), I figure the creek is now low enough to cross. Using my hiking sticks, I gingerly work my way across the stream without falling.

"YEAH! I'm across!" My triumphant cries echo through the misty valley. One hurdle is crossed. Nice work, Talie!

Ummm….now what?

Why would an otherwise sane, 60 year old, American woman put herself in this dangerous situation? Because I simply love it! Sure, I might not say that I love it when things are this scary, but what a challenge it is to face what Mother Nature throws at you and come out on top. I love to "push my envelope" because when I have finished an extreme adventure like this one, I feel alive. I feel fearless and invincible. It's a feeling that grows on you!

The stories in this book are not for beginner hikers. I have been going into the backcountry for years, and have learned my lessons through many experiences - some good, some uncomfortable. These are just a few of the adventures I have had since I turned 60 in 2006. I want to show you that it is possible to continue to push your limits and enjoy solo backpacking during your 60s decade….and beyond. When I was young, I thought 60 would be "old". But now I have finished that decade, I have found that by staying strong and focused I can have a wonderful time backpacking and adventuring and I aim to continue into my 70s.

How did I get Here?

• • •

GOING SOLO, BEING SAFE, STAYING IN TOUCH

But if you judge safety to be the paramount consideration in life you should never, under any circumstances, go on long hikes alone. Don't take short hikes alone, either – or, for that matter, go anywhere alone. And avoid at all costs such foolhardy activities as driving, falling in love, or inhaling air that is almost certainly riddled with deadly germs. Wear wool next to the skin. Insure every good and chattel you possess against every conceivable contingency the future might bring, even if the premiums half-cripple the present. Never cross an intersection against a red light, even when you can see all roads are clear for miles. And never, of course, explore the guts of an idea that seems as if it might threaten one of your more cherished beliefs. In your wisdom you will probably live to be a ripe old age. But you may discover, just before you die, that you have been dead for a long, long time.

Colin Fletcher, The Complete Walker

MY LOVE OF THE OUTDOORS has always been with me, but my passion for backpacking and camping was developed when, as a child, I went to summer camp. Then as an adult (ha!), I spent many years as wife and mother (and now grandmother). Those were some of the best years of my life! But then when my children grew up and took off on their own, I could once again put together my solo adventures.

Why do I go solo? Now that's a good question! Henry David Thoreau put it this way: *the man who goes alone can start today; but he who travels with another must wait till that other is ready.*

When I am solo in the wilderness, I am just plain happy. I can go as slow as I want, take as many photos as I want, and just stop and listen to the silence of the forest whenever I want. Sometimes, I listen to my footsteps as they hit the trail. I can't let my mind wander too much, as that can be dangerous, but I can feel my steps and listen to my breath as I walk. It becomes a form of meditation for me.

Being solo, I am so aware of my surroundings. Sometimes this is necessary to stay safe, but often I am just taking in the beauty of the forest. I notice the colors, the flowers and trees, the rocks, the small animals, even bugs on the trail. I become super aware that I am just a small part of the greater scheme of things out here. I am just passing through. A visitor. A guest of Mother Nature.

Solo backpacking has many small steps to master before you take off for a multi-day trip. I have refined my gear until it is as light as possible for someone in their 70s! I have a knowledge base that includes being trained as an Emergency Medical Technician. I have spent many years on Crested Butte Search and Rescue, training with them, and going on missions to find and help people. But I think the most useful skill in the backcountry is common sense. It is important to keep calm, look at the whole situation, and think clearly about solutions. As they say in the search and rescue world: *Safety comes from good judgment, good judgment comes from experience, and experience comes from bad judgment."*

Completing a difficult and challenging adventure in the wilderness is an achievement and it is even more rewarding when I do it solo. Many people think that going solo is just looking for trouble. They ask me a lot of "what if" questions:

What if you hurt yourself?
What if you get lost?
What if you meet a wild animal?
What if that wild animal is really hungry???

If I was to lead my life thinking about all these "what ifs", I wouldn't have a fraction of the fun I am having now. Part of the challenge of managing the "what ifs" is to minimize the risk. I think I have the wisdom to make good decisions. I have the experience to pay attention and hopefully not get lost. I have the knowledge of first aid to deal with injuries. I have the good sense to carry a locator beacon. It boils down to looking at the risks, weighing the possibilities, and then deciding if I want to continue.

Another thing I love about being solo is the added dimension of anticipation. Being with someone else is a little safer, a little easier. By being on my own, I have to rely on myself. There is anticipation and concentration that I don't get when others are present. I know that if anything goes wrong, it is my fault, and my fault alone. It's up to me to fix the situation.

Each of us has what I call an "envelope of safety" - that place where you feel safe and secure. Each time I start a difficult adventure, I know I am pushing my own safety envelope pretty far out there. I have likened it to standing on the end of a diving board, getting ready to jump, and really hoping there is water in the pool! But that one leap of faith, not knowing if there is water, can change your life.

The wonders of modern technology have given us a great deal of safety netting. For example, I used to hire an EPRB (Emergency Personal Rescue Beacon). I now have my own SPOT locator beacon. This little guy will send a message to a satellite that will then show up on a web site. My children and friends can go online and see where I am. I usually only turn it on at night for about 30 minutes, long enough for them to see that I have moved from where I was the night before. If I should get into a life or death situation, I can push the SOS button and it will alert the Search and Rescue authorities.

Then I discovered GPS devices. To have a small item that not only has all your maps on it, but also shows where on the map you are is wonderfully reassuring. I might not have gotten lost in Tasmania if I had had a GPS. More on that later...

When Kindle readers came out, I was so excited! I was able to read 15 books on my Pyrenees trip with no extra weight. And even though I was in France, Spain and Andorra, I could get books in English. Oh, how I remember the days of wandering around European cities looking for an English bookstore. I also remember re-reading the same book over and over because I couldn't find a new one in English!

In the Pyrenees, I carried my SPOT, my Kindle, my GPS and my camera, along with my iPhone. But in the few years between my Pyrenees hike and my Colorado Trail hike, which you'll read about shortly, most of those items have been combined into my iPhone. In the Pyrenees, I was always looking for a place to buy batteries for the GPS. Now, I simply carry a light-weight solar charger. On the 41 days of the Colorado Trail, there was just one night when I couldn't bring my phone up to 100% charge. And because I had my iPhone with me on the Colorado Trail, when I was in cell range, I was able to text my re-suppliers, letting them know if I was on, or ahead, of schedule. What an interesting time to be a backpacker!

Being in the wilderness is a special experience for me, each and every time. My heart swells with the love I feel for Mother Nature. There is a relationship we seem to have. I feel truly loved and accepted, part of the grand scheme of things, as a sister of the trees, rocks, and mountains! I never think I'm lonely. I believe that Mother Nature doesn't give us any right or wrongs. She doesn't tell us what we should do. However, there are definite consequences of our actions, so I need to pay close attention.

I once met someone on the trail who told me I was very courageous. My response was: "Courageous or crazy?" I guess there is a fine line between them. Where is that line? And, really, which side of it am I on? Where I think the line falls between the two is: You are "courageous" until something goes wrong. And then you suddenly become "crazy".

After all is said and done, there is potentially a situation where I won't be saved. Am I ok with that? Yes! I have had a wonderful life, and at 70 I have seen many beautiful and awe-inspiring places. We are all going to transition out of this life sometime, and I hope to make it into my 90's. I will continue to go solo backpacking for as long as I am able. If something should happen to me, and I am not able to rescue myself, I am willing to take responsibility for the consequences. I have even told my kids that if I should not come back sometime, "Please know I was doing what I love."

New Zealand

● ● ●

My life has no purpose, no direction, no aim, no meaning, and
yet I'm happy. I can't figure it out. What am I doing right?

Charles Schultz

SINCE I WAS BORN IN 1946, 2006 is the year I turned 60. My birthday is in June, but I thought I would start this decade of adventures with the start of 2006. That year, I was in one of my favorite places on the planet: New Zealand. This was my 4th trip to New Zealand (as I write this I think I am into my 11th trip!). The summer down there is from December to April – so it is a great get-a-way from the Northern Hemisphere. I had a pretty busy couple of months that year (I guess I was "young" at 60!). I am starting out with these 5 adventures in 2006.

Early January 2006

Three Tarns Pass?

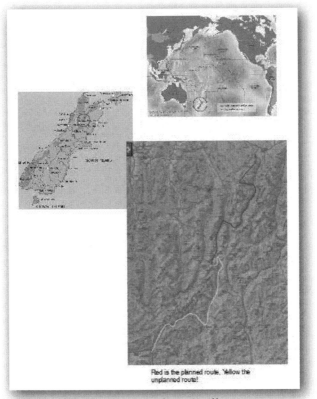

Red is the planned route, Yellow the unplanned route!

For more detail on maps, go to: http://still-going-strong.com

This New Zealand adventure (part of which is in the introduction) started on a lovely and warm December day (actually in 2005). I was in the St. Arnaud Department of Conservation (DoC) office, looking at a giant wall map of the Nelson Lakes area. I asked a young woman who was behind the desk, "Is it possible to walk from St. Arnard to Lewis Pass?"

"Oh," she said. "You need to talk to Simon!" A few minutes later, out bounded Simon, another DoC employee, armed with lots of enthusiasm and ideas. But he really hooked me when he showed me a spot on the map with three small lakes. He called it "Three Tarns Pass" (back then the map didn't even have it named). After 30 minutes with Simon, I had my plan:

Hike up to the Angeles Hut (Night One) – From there I would go to the Upper Travis Hut (Night Two) - Then, over the Travers Saddle down to the West Sabine Hut (Night Three)- Up to the Blue Lake Hut (Night Four)- Over Waiau Pass, to camp at Thompson Lake (Night Five)- Over Thompson Pass, down to the East Matakitaki – only a possibility of a hut (Night Six) - Up the West Matakitaki, to Bob's Hut (Night Seven)- Over Three Tarns Pass, down to Ada Pass Hut (Night Eight), and finally ending up at Lewis Pass.

A GREAT plan! It would probably take me nine days of backpacking, and I always took one extra day of food in case I got stranded. That made for a reasonably heavy pack, but I figured, if I planned it right, I should be able to carry everything.

Now, all packed up, I hired a personal locator beacon and arranged transport from the DoC office (where there was a relatively safe place to leave my van) to the Robert's Ridge trailhead. Hiking up Roberts Ridge was a demanding climb even without a heavy pack, so it was pretty slow going. But by the end of the day, I was at the Angeles Hut. I love this hut. It's located in a beautiful little cirque high up in those spectacular New Zealand mountains.

On the second day, I hiked the Cascade Track. An enjoyable part of my journey, as it was DOWN hill! Next was the hike up to the Upper Travers, also smooth sailing. This part of the track went along a river so it was relatively flat. I passed the John Tate Hut at midday and stopped to have lunch. From the John Tate, the track became a little more of a climb until I got to the Upper Travers Hut.

When I arrived, I took my pack off on the porch while I removed my boots. It is considered good etiquette to remove your wet, muddy footwear before going into a hut. The hut was almost full. As a slow hiker, I was one of the last to get to the hut, but there was still a bunk available, so I claimed my sleeping place, unpacked my cooking gear and food, and headed out to the common room.

As I sat down, I was swarmed by other trampers. They had all sorts of questions for me! It seems that when I had put down my pack to remove my boots, they had noticed all the patches on it: Kilimanjaro, Crested Butte Search and Rescue, Alaska, New Zealand (of course), and Wales. Those patches were a great conversation starter!

On Day Three, I went up and over the Travers Saddle and got to West Sabine Hut relatively early. Rather than stop for the night, I decided to push on to the Blue Lake Hut. Before I left the West Sabine, the DoC hut warden mentioned that a storm with gale force winds was expected in a couple of days. Maybe I should have paid more attention to his warning...

By the time I got to Blue Lake Hut that night, I was pretty tired. Skipping a hut had seemed like a good idea at the time, but by the end of the day, I was re-thinking that decision. Since the next day was New Year's Eve, I decided to take a rest day. I was a day ahead of schedule after skipping the West Sabine Hut, plus there were three cute Kiwi guys at the Blue Lake Hut: Chris, Max and Towhai. They were fun to hang out with, so we spent New Year's Eve day exploring the rocks around Lake Constance, just above the Blue Lake Hut, before hiking over to some large waterfalls.

Towhai and Max got into the pool and let the water come crashing down on their heads. Chris had a new Gore-Tex jacket and wanted to test it, so he put it on and went out under the waterfall. It kept him dry for about a minute, he figured! I had a great time watching them get soaked, while I stayed dry. It was a lovely way to end 2005.

When I realized I could see Waiau Pass from where I was sitting, I got a little nervous. "Yikes," I thought, "that's where I'm going tomorrow!" It looked steep and intimidating. I didn't want to dwell on it and spoil the fun I was having with the Kiwi guys, so I just put it out of my mind and told myself I would deal with that problem tomorrow.

There was almost a full hut at Blue Lake that New Year's Eve, but luckily no one wanted a noisy celebration. I had a long day ahead of me, so I didn't even stay up to see in the New Year!

Very early on New Year's Day 2006, there I was climbing the moraine wall to get back to Lake Constance. I had to hike high above the side of the lake in order to miss some cliffs that were next to the water. It wasn't well marked and I ended up going too high and had to hike back down, which added an hour or so to the day. It was frustrating, because I was expending energy that could be better used on the pass. Then I had a steep descent through a gully to get back to the lake edge.

I followed the valley floor above the lake, and found the track on the true right of the river (in Crested Butte lingo, we would say "skier's right"). The track headed up into loose rock and gravel. It was really steep! Loose rock can be tricky sometimes - you take one step up and then slide two steps back down!

The pass that had me so scared the day before was not nearly as bad as it had looked. Things often seem to look worse from afar than they actually are. As I neared the summit, the track was not so steep and the scree turned to tussocks. By late morning I was on top of Waiau Pass! I had a clear view over Lake Constance to the north, the Waiau Valley to the south, and the Thompson Pass to the west. Below Thompson Pass, I could see the lovely little Thompson Lake, where I planned to camp for the night.

After taking a few photos at the pass, I headed down the other side. There was supposed to be a marked route, but I sure couldn't find it. It was just as steep as the other side had been. This was one of those times where it was harder to find a route going down a slope, than it was going up it. And once you were off the route, you had to be especially careful of not getting "cliffed out": when the trail ends up at a cliff which is too steep to climb down. But by careful maneuvering, I made it down to the valley floor without mishap.

The marked route on my map showed a trail going down the Waiau River, but I knew I was not on that route as I was headed to Thompson Pass. So now, I was on my own with no trail. But since I had seen Thompson Lake, and the pass above it from the top of Waiau Pass, I had some idea of where I was going. It was a really steep climb to the lake and it had been a rather tough day.

When I got to the lake, it was only 4:00pm, but I was very tired. I found a little camping spot next to the lake, where a big rock protected one side. Someone had built rock walls on two sides of it, creating a sheltered spot. This was a perfect place to put up my tarp and settle in for the night. That is, I would have been protected if the winds were coming from the right direction. But they weren't! Remember the storm warning the ranger had given me at the West Sabine Hut? Well, it was about to hit...

When the storm actually came in at about 4:00am, the winds changed direction. My little shelter no longer protected me, and was actually funneling the wind and rain right onto me. The winds were gale force! Ever tried to rest under a flapping, flopping, shaking tarp? Not really conducive to sleep. So I basically wrapped myself up in the tarp in order to stop it from flapping (in backpacking lingo this is called "taco-ing"). I guess it was about 5:00am when I realized my feet were getting wet in what was supposed to be my water-resistant sleeping bag. Uh oh!

By now, you'll recognize this as the little predicament I mentioned at the start of the book.

Later that day, when I had finally crossed the swollen creek, it was 8:00 pm and everything I had, including my sleeping bag, was wet. Setting up a camp wouldn't really help me stay warm and dry, as I would just get cold again. I guessed I should just keep walking. Unlike step aerobics, I'd actually be getting somewhere, and not staying in one place.

As it started to get dark, I knew it would be hard to navigate. But after checking with my map, I figured that all I needed to do was to keep the river on my right. I didn't need to see it – because I could hear the river and know how close to it I was. Oh, having a GPS back then would have been a joy...but hindsight is a wonderful thing!

Hiking at night was an eerie experience. My whole world was a small circle lit up from my headlamp. It was slow going. There wasn't a real trail that I could see, and walking by headlamp made it hard to find faint hunting or fishing trails.

There was supposed to be a bivy shelter along the way - Caroline Bivy. I did look for it, but I must have passed it in the dark. Since a wilderness bivy doesn't have a heat source it probably wouldn't have done me much good anyway.

About 3:00am, I stopped for a snack, thinking how interesting this night walking was. It was surreal! Then, at about 5:00am, things started getting faintly light. It was great to have some visual concept of the mountains. And I loved hearing the birds wake up and start singing. It was a crisp, clear morning after a long, dark night.

I thought I had gone a lot further during the night than I actually had. So, it took me quite a while to orientate myself on the map. As is often the case when you are using map and compass, there is a tendency to try to make the land around you fit the map. I am embarrassed to admit that I spent a couple of hours trying to do just that.

Finally I said to myself, "Ok, time to stop, fix a cup of tea, and re-orient myself." Once I did that, I saw where on the map I really was, and how far I still had to go. It was not a happy realization. I had been awake for over 24 hours, and had to be extra careful not to let sleep deprivation cloud my judgment. I was so sleep deprived that I occasionally fell asleep standing up, leaning on my hiking poles!

I was still moving down the valley when I saw a wonderful sight: The Christopher Hut! To make this vision even more wonderful, there was smoke coming out of the chimney! As I stumbled in at about 4:00pm, I joined 11 members of the Auckland Baptist Hiking Club. What beautiful people. They helped me hang my soggy sleeping bag above the wood stove. Then they filled me with tea and hot soup. I would have to sleep on the floor since all the bunks were taken, but there was an extra mattress and I was overjoyed to be somewhere warm and dry.

The next day was the perfect opportunity to take a rest day, and give my swollen feet time to recover. Looking out from the hut, I was amazed to see how much snow there was in the high country where I had been. I was lucky I got down when I did.

After my rest day at the Christopher Hut, I left at 8:15 the following morning. I was hiking, with dry gear, in the daylight, and on a trail! I had renewed gratitude for those simple things.

I got to the Ada Pass Hut in time for lunch, and then on to the Cannibal Gorge Hut for the night. It took a while to get the coal stove burning, and it never seemed to get very warm. I was joined in the hut by Jill and Jan, two fun ladies from England and New Zealand. I taught them how to play my little game of Farkle, and they loved it.

I left early next morning and arrived at Lewis Pass at 10:20am. I still needed to hitchhike back to St. Arnaud to get to my van. It was cold and windy as I tried to get a ride. I would pull my hood up to stay warm, but when a car came by, I'd push it off my head and smile, hoping that would help get a ride. The kind people who eventually stopped told me they had never picked up a hitchhiker before, but as I looked so cold, they decided to come back and pick me up!

It took two more rides to get back to St. Arnaud. After returning the rescue beacon, doing some laundry and taking a hot shower, I felt like a new woman. I was a slightly frustrated woman too. Sure, I had walked from St. Arnaud to Lewis Pass. That was my original goal and I did complete it. BUT, what about Three Tarns Pass?? Because of the storm, and me changing my route as a result, I had missed Thompson Pass, the East Matakitaki, the West Matakitaki, and Three Tarns Pass. I was both elated and disappointed. But we could rectify that, right?

After this aborted Three Tarns Pass hike, I drove up to Nelson to visit a friend. While I was there, I bought a waterproof bivy stack. Does this sounds like closing the barn door after the horse got out?

Starting off up Robert's Ridge

Lake Angeles

Blue Lake

Travers Saddle

Waiou Pass Looking toward Thompson Lake

Camp at Thompson Lake - Before the storm!

Snow on the tops after the storm!

For more photos go to: http://still-going-strong.com

Mid-January 2006

Three Tarn Pass – Unfinished Business

"There is no dishonor in losing the race," Don said. "There is only dishonor in not racing because you are afraid to lose."

Garth Stein, The Art of Racing in the Rain

Of course, I still wanted to see this place called Three Tarns Pass. It had become somewhat mystical to me. So back I went to the St. Arnaud DoC office, where the girls now knew me by name. I once again checked the big map on the wall. I saw that I could go up a different drainage (the D'Urville River) and over a different pass (David's Saddle) and still get to the area I had missed: the East Matakitaki, the West Matakitaki, Bob's hut, and Three Tarns Pass.

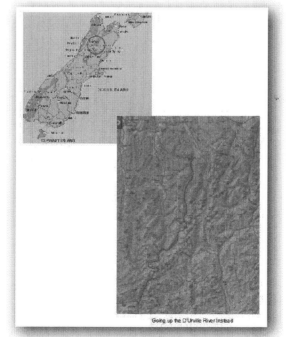

Going up the D'Urville River instead

For more detail on maps, go to: http://still-going-strong.com

So, mid-January, I was off again to the grocery store to restock. This route looked like it would cut a day off the trip, so I didn't need quite as much food. But that reduced weight was replaced by my new bivy sack. It was heavier than my simple tarp, but at least it would keep me drier. I hired another locator beacon, and arranged a shuttle to the trailhead. I was on the trail at noon.

I passed the first hut, Speargrass Hut, and went on to the Sabine Hut that evening. This was interesting, because every other time I had been at the Sabine Hut, I was at the end of the Travers Circuit. This time I was just starting a trip. After a night at the hut, I headed over to the d'Urville River at 7:40am.

I was a little concerned about having to cross both the Sabine and the D'Urville rivers. I knew there was a bridge over the Sabine, but the D'Urville didn't have one. Luckily, I was able to cross at a shallow part of the river. There was a hut at the river mouth, but I continued up the trail to the Morgan Hut, getting there at 2:15 pm. It was a little early to stop, but it was starting to rain. I was joined in the hut by three young fishermen from the Netherlands, and then by a couple from Sweden.

It was still raining the next morning, but I packed up anyway and hiked to the Ella Hut (since renamed as George Lyon Hut). I had checked the forecast, and it was supposed to rain all day. I decided to stop at the Ella and wait for the weather to pass. Maybe I was not as hard-headed as I thought? And by now, it was raining buckets!

Spending 24 hours in a hut by yourself is interesting. I had a book, but it wasn't long before I had read the whole thing. I had some cards, and there were several games of solitaire I knew. That took up a little more time. And I had a dice game called "Farkle"; I'd even figured out how to play solitaire Farkle! So I had plenty to entertain myself. At least I was dry in the hut, rather than walking in the rain.

New Zealand huts often have a heat source. In the Ella Hut, it was a small wood stove. I split a little wood, but the rain had made everything damp and it was hard to get a fire started. So, I made some fire-starters. I took a blank piece of paper from my book, and tore it in half. Then I took some candle drippings from the candleholders in the hut, and shaved them into the paper. Using a lit candle, I melted these little pieces together and crumpled up the paper. When the paper was lit, it burned for a long time because of the wax, and thus I got the fire started without using so many little sticks.

By the next morning, I was stir crazy! It was still cloudy, but only raining a little. The trail looked like a lake, but I wasn't up to staying another day in the Ella Hut. I figured that if the storm continued, I could always stop in the Upper D'Urville Hut. As I left the hut, I saw a patch of blue sky peek through the clouds. After an hour of hiking, the clouds were parting and blue sky was taking over.

It took an hour to get up to the bridge which goes over to Moss Pass (another route to Blue Lake), and four hours to get to the Upper D'Urville Bivy. I met three guys coming down from the bivy - they were doing my route, but in the opposite direction. So the Upper D'Urville Hut wasn't a hut after all, but a cute little two bunk bivy.

My first look at David's Saddle was mind-boggling. It looked very steep, and just getting to it looked daunting. Remember how I said the same thing about the Waiau Pass? I reminded myself that it usually wasn't as bad as it looked. I had orange triangles to follow uphill into a small gully. Then, it became hand over hand climbing to come out above a waterfall. I found myself in a field of Wild Spaniards above the waterfall. Before I could get to the scree of the saddle, I had some "dancing" to do! Wild Spaniards are beautiful plants that grow in the high country. They have a yellow blooming stalk, and very sharp pointed leaves. When you get close to a Wild Spaniard, you know it! I have had them draw blood through a pair of pants, so I danced and dodged my way around them the best I could. After dancing with the Wild Spaniards, I got into some lovely tussocks and then reached the scree of David's Saddle. It was a fairly easy zig-zag to get to the top.

Oh, what a view! I could see all the way down two drainages. I was directly between the D'Urville River drainage which I had come up, and the East Matakitaki River drainage where I would be going. I kept looking one way and thinking it was the most beautiful view, then I would look the opposite direction and think *that* was the most beautiful view. In each drainage, I could see the river snaking its way down between the mountains. Part of the joy of being on top of a pass is the hard work it took to get there, but just being able to see such sights always makes my heart sing.

I knew I had better get off the pass and find a place to camp before it got dark. On the Matakitaki side of David's Saddle, it was loose and steep, with no markers or track to follow. I had to be careful not to slip on the steep stuff. In New Zealand, some of the high steep hills are covered with a grass referred to as "snow grass". It grows close to the ground and is very slippery. Because it is on very steep terrain, you can easily slip and slide down the slope, so I had to be totally aware of where I was putting my feet.

After an hour and a half, I found a relatively level spot at the spring, which was the start of the Matakitaki River, and plopped down for the day. For this high mountain camp, I had my new Alpine Bivy Bag, along with my tarp. Of course, because I had all this gear to keep me dry, it didn't rain! Not that I was complaining. I witnessed a spectacular sunset and a star-filled sky that night. I was in one of the most remote places I had ever been, and I was loving it.

The next day, I bush bashed down the East Matakitaki for an hour or so before I found a trail. After another couple of hours, I came to a junction where I had to go up the West Matakitaki. My choices involved going across a three-wire bridge, or wading through the stream a little further down. The bridge was rather high up, and I was still a bit of a bridge novice back then, so I chose to wade through the stream.

It was a bit of a climb through the bush as I hiked up the valley, then down again to the flats and Bob's Hut. Someone had built a pretend grave with a cross on it that said "Bob". Got to love that droll Kiwi humor. I was the only one at Bob's Hut – the further out into the wilderness I got, the fewer people I saw. Actually I hadn't seen anyone since the Sabine Hut. It didn't worry me at all. I was reveling in this isolation!

Early the next morning, I started out on a track along the Matakitaki River, which got smaller and smaller as I went higher and higher. I think most of these river tracks were made by fishermen, because once the stream gets so small that big fish aren't in it anymore, the track ends! Not having a track wasn't really a problem; it just meant my travel was quite a bit slower. However, I did miss the place where I was supposed to go up to avoid a gorge and had to do some horrendous bush bashing until I could get above it.

Once it opened up, I was in and out of the creek, which was no longer big enough to count as a river. Along the banks there were plenty of Wild Spaniards, and as gorgeous as they were, I didn't feel like getting bloody from their jabs. So after a while, I just stayed in the creek!

There were all sorts of large daisies blooming along the creek and amongst the tussocks. When you get to these high mountain areas, there are many herbaceous flowering plants growing between the snow tussocks. Among them are numerous species of mountain daisy, Spaniard, buttercup, eyebright and gentian. Compared with continental alpine areas, the flowering season in New Zealand is prolonged. Some buttercup and marsh marigold species are in full flower from November to December, daisies bloom from December to March with a peak in January, and gentians flower from late January into April. I was there in the height of the bloom-ing season, and it was quite a sight.

From my map, I could see that the creek went up to the tarns, so I knew I was going the right way. So up, up, up I went - steeper and steeper, slower and slower. I had all day to get there and I wasn't in any rush. I felt like a little kid hiking up the creek, hopping from boulder to boulder. It was a little discouraging that the creek kept going around a large hill. I couldn't see where it was going to end, and I felt like I would be climbing forever. Finally, the gully went into a waterfall, and I knew I needed to climb out of the creek bed. With a little bit of scrambling, and some more dancing with the Wild Spaniards, I came up on some flats, and there - FINALLY - were The Three Tarns! I had made it up there in five hours, and it was only 1:00pm. I had time to hang out, and enjoy the sunshine.

I drank some of the pure water, and filled my water bottles. This is special water to me, and I still have a little bottle of it in my storage locker in Crested Butte! The tarns were pretty big for "tarns", but I wasn't about to call them lakes. The shelf I was on was incredible. Steep jagged peaks all around, with rocks and scree coming down to the lakes' edges. And the tarns draining off the shelf making the waterfall and stream I had come up. What a spectacular high mountain spot! There was still snow tucked around the peaks, and snow grass and tussocks growing where ever it could get some roots down, but mostly it was a rocky steep basin, with three little lakes in it. Yea – I had made it to the Three Tarns! I was elated!

I spent some time reconnoitering my route from there. According to my description, what looked the easiest way up was not necessarily the best way. The real pass was up a fairly narrow "gut" of scree. As is my wont, I couldn't sit and think about it too much, because I would just get more scared. "So", I said to myself, "just start doing it, Talie" – and up I went. It sure was steep! And it was pretty loose rock - one step up, then one step sliding back down. I often felt like all the rocks above me would come tumbling down as I scrambled up. But I worked my way up this notch in the mountain, and before I knew it, there I was on top of the actual Three Tarns Pass. I think this was, and still is, my favorite place on the planet! It was well worth the effort that it had taken me to get there!

From the pass, I looked down on the Three Tarns. I could see them better from above than when I was actually level with them. Looking back the way I had come was the Matakitaki drainage, but the hill I had climbed around was blocking the view down valley, so it was all rocks and scree and mountains as far as I could see. But when I looked in the other direction, towards where I was going, there were layers and layers of mountain peaks and passes. I was also looking down on another tarn on that side of the pass. Best of all, when I turned back around, I was looking down again on the Three Tarns. It had been a long and arduous couple of weeks getting here, and I was feeling the joy of having fulfilled my goal.

There was a lot of scree scrambling to get down off the pass, but it wasn't as steep as the one I had just come up. From the edge of this new tarn's shelf, I could look down the drainage and see Ada Pass. It was not going to be an easy descent, but at least it was in a downward direction. I am often happier when I am going down, but it actually can be harder on your body, especially your knees. I followed the stream most of the way, until I got to the edge of the bush. Then it got a bit more difficult as I made my way through the trees and down to the river.

Once I crossed the river, I climbed up onto the St. James Walkway track at Ada Pass. When I had been here a couple of weeks before I was cold and wet, but this time I was on Cloud Nine. Tired, yes, but elated! From the pass, it was a short walk to the Ada Pass Hut. An 11-hour day, with some pretty serious altitude gain and loss, so I was a happy but exhausted tramper.

After a blissful night's sleep, I left at about 7:00am, passing by the Cannibal Gorge Hut. I poked my head in, but the trampers there were still sleeping. I continued on, crossing the Maruia River on the swing bridge. I met a group of kids and adults coming in from Lewis Pass and they loved my story of where I had been. The sleepers in the Cannibal Gorge Hut were their friends, so they had a laugh about them still sleeping!

I got to Lewis Pass about 12:30pm, and started to hitch back to St. Arnaud. It was pretty painless, even if it again took three different rides. The last ride was with two guys in a camper van, and we ended up camping next to each other at the campground at Lake Rotoiti. I think they appreciated me more after I had showered and put on clean clothes!

Before I got to the campground, I stopped at the store and bought some juice and cookies for the girls at the DoC office. When I returned the locator beacon, they were almost as excited as I was about completing the hike over Three Tarns Pass!

For more photos go to: http://still-going-strong.com

February 2006

Dusky Track

Solo wilderness travel - if it's your bag - offers priceless bonuses. But it imposes constraints, when you're traveling alone, if you've got any sense, you exercise a tinge more care than if you had company. Any mistake is likely to prove serious; a major mistake will likely be your last.

Colin Fletcher, *The Man Who Walked Through Time*

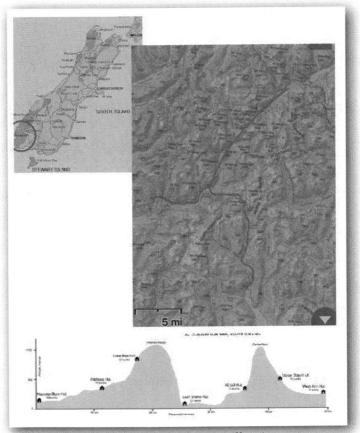

For more detail on maps, go to: http://still-going-strong.com

The Dusky Track: This difficult tramping track between Lake Hauroko and Lake Manapouri offers huge lakes, gushing rivers, vast forested valleys and lots of mud for experienced and well equipped trampers.
Highlights:

> * *It crosses three major valley systems and two mountain ranges.*
> * *Offers fantastic views over a vast Fiordland landscape.*

Is difficult but rewarding.
Dusky Sound, one of the largest fiords in New Zealand, was named by Captain James Cook on his first voyage to New Zealand in 1770. He did not enter the fiord because it was getting dark and so named it Dusky Sound.
The first explorer to try and map an overland route to Dusky Sound was Sir Thomas Mackenzie in 1894 and 1896. In 1903, when jobs were scarce, about 50 West Coast miners were set to work building a track from Supper Cove to Lake Manapouri. Living in tent camps, the men endured sand flies and rain for a reward of twelve and sixpence a day, plus food.
The track, still clearly evident for much of its length, was cut six feet wide with a drain on one side. It extended to a point just past where the Loch Maree hut stands today. Picks, crowbars and a hefty anvil still lie at the side of the track, just above Loch Maree, where the men left them when work came to a halt.

Department of Conservation Brochure

When I embarked on my Dusky Sound Adventure I was on my fourth trip to New Zealand. One of my goals was to hike the Dusky Track. Having just completed Three Tarns Pass, I thought the Dusky would be a good follow up.

The Dusky Track is, quite simply, one of the most amazing walks in New Zealand. It's 84 kilometers long, straight through the heart of Fiordland National Park. It starts at Lake Hauroko, goes all the way to

Dusky Sound, then back out to Lake Manapouri. The Dusky is supposedly the hardest established track in Fiordland. I had heard how hard it was – everyone talked about all the mud on it! So, of course, I was eager to do it! All the literature I read said NOT to do it alone, so that summer I asked my friends and everyone I met on the trails if they wanted to do the Dusky with me. Most people would say, "The Dusky? I have heard how muddy that one is! No way!" So I really did try to find someone to do it with me, but to no avail. By now, you know me somewhat and shouldn't be surprised that I decided to go solo anyway. Why not? How hard could it be?

I drove to Te Anau, my favorite Kiwi town. I spent a day getting my gear and food organized for an eight-day trip. Plus, I hired an EPLB (Locator Beacon) from the petrol station. (I never could figure out why Search and Rescue chose petrol stations to rent out locator beacons!)

I also needed to arrange transport to get to the start of the trip. As the track starts at Lake Hauroko, and ends at Lake Manapouri, I had to figure out how to leave my van at the end and get taken to the beginning. One option was a floatplane leaving from Te Anau and landing on Lake Hauroko, but that was a bit pricy. My next option was to park at the town of Manapouri, take van transport down to Clifton where I could get a lift to the lake, followed by a boat ride across the lake. That way, my van would be waiting for me at the end of the trip, and it was not quite as expensive as flying.

I called the company that went across Lake Hauroko and spoke to the owner. He had a scheduled crossing two days a week and he could pick me up where the bus let me off in Clifton. Great! When he asked how many people to expect, I said, "Just one. Me." There was hesitation on the other end of the line, then he said he didn't think he could take me. I asked why not, and he said I shouldn't do the Dusky alone. Aargh! Here we go again! So, I spent a few minutes telling him I that I was a member of Search and

Rescue back home, that I had been a guide for the last 15 years, that I had a locator beacon with me, and that I was perfectly capable of doing The Dusky solo. It took a bit to convince him, but finally he agreed, even if he wasn't totally happy about it.

I drove to Manapouri, ready for an early morning pick up. The bus took me to Clifton, where I switched to a truck. We drove to where Val, the boat company owner, stored his boat, hooked it to the back of his truck, and drove the rest of the way to Lake Hauroko – about 30 minutes on a dirt road.

Lake Hauroko is located in a mountain valley in Fiordland National Park. The S-shaped lake is 30 kilometers in length and is New Zealand's deepest lake at 425 meters. That's even deeper than Lake Superior in the USA. There are mountain peaks surrounding the lake, with thick bush coming right down to the edge of the water.

Once Val's boat was ready to go, I gathered up my pack and climbed aboard. As we got out on the lake, it became really rough. I stood next to Val in the front of the boat and tried to let my knees take the shocks of each wave. It took us about 45 minutes to get across the lake. It was a LONG 45 minutes, but it sure was beautiful!

We finally arrived at the beach in front of the Hauroko Burn Hut. I put on my pack, thanked Val, and hopped ashore. I was instantly swarmed by sandflies. I couldn't get out my bug repellant fast enough!

I poked my head into the DoC hut at the lake edge. I thought it might be good to have an early lunch before I started up the trail, and at least I'd be protected from the sandflies by being in the hut. Not! They were in there too. No long lunch for this lady. I made it short and was on my way. I could hardly wait to get away from the beach and the sandflies. Those little guys can make you pretty miserable. Besides, my DoC brochure said that from the lake to the first hut was a four to six hour hike. I am usually a bit of a slow hiker, so I assumed it would take me longer than that. I had better be on my way!

Fiordland is one of the wettest areas in the world. Some parts receive eight meters of rain a year. The mountains are just off the ocean facing the prevailing westerly winds, so the moisture-laden air has to rise to move past the peaks, where the moisture condenses and falls as rain. There aren't many places in the world with this combination. That amount of water can create swollen rivers and muddy tracks, but also some of the most lush forests and mosses. Without all that the rain, Fiordland just wouldn't be Fiordland.

The first part of the trail followed the Hauroko Burn. ("Burn" is a Scottish or Northern English name for a small stream.) The stream treated me to glimpses of pools with reflections of ferns and trees. I loved the sound of the water running beside me. Thankfully, the river wasn't high, so I didn't need to use the first three wire bridge. The trail was well marked with the standard plastic orange triangles nailed to occasional trees. Then it started gaining altitude, which dramatically slowed my progress. Mid-afternoon, I stopped and took my pack off for a snack. It felt so good to put the pack down, even for just a few minutes. Finally, after almost eight hours of hiking, I reached the Halfway Hut at 6:45pm. There were plenty of sandflies to greet me, inside and outside the hut. When it got dark, the sandflies went to sleep. But as they went to sleep, the mosquitos woke up. Good thing I had lots of bug repellant for this trip.

Since leaving Val at the lake, I had not seen anyone. I was all alone in the hut that night. I figured that was pretty unusual since this was such a well-known trek. I enjoy being in a hut by myself so it was no big deal that no one was there. Since no one else had started the track at the same time as me, it looked like I might really be doing this whole adventure solo! Unless, of course, I caught up with someone ahead of me, or someone behind me caught up with me - a real possibility. Whether there would be others on the track with me or not, I was happy to finally be hiking the Dusky.

The next day, I would have quite a bit of elevation to gain so I figured it would be a long day. It was listed as a three to five hour hike, but as I would be going up, I felt I'd need the whole day to get to the Lake Roe Hut, so I left the Halfway Hut at 8:15am.

After a couple of hours, I came to my first three-wire bridge. A three-wire bridge is just what it says: three wires in a bit of a triangle. To get from one side of a river to the other, you walk on one wire, while holding onto the other two. There are support poles along the way which keep the whole thing together, and often an extra wire to keep it from swinging too much. If the wires are high in the air, you first have to climb a ladder to get up on the bridge. That can be a bit tricky to start with because you have to balance on a ladder with a full backpack, and then wiggle your way between the top wires until your feet are on the bottom wire. I was also worried about the mud coating on my boots - I didn't want my feet to slip off the wire.

I hike with two hiking poles and they'd often get in the way of the bridge supports. So I would loop the poles on my wrists, scoot along to the first support, swing my poles past the supports, and continue on. I don't particularly like "exposure" in high places, and a three wire bridge is total exposure! When crossing a three wire bridge, I wouldn't think about how far down it was, or how fast the river was flowing. Keeping my boots centered on that little wire, and supporting myself with the other two wires, was all I could think of. I soon became pretty good at three-wire bridges. On my nine-day trip, I crossed 21 of them!

Because I was in Fiordland, it was very lush. Trees covered with mosses, ferns of every description and green underbrush were everywhere I looked. But all these plants have roots, and often the track was nothing more than a maze of roots, which was totally challenging …as if the tracks weren't challenging enough! New Zealand's trail builders are not known for putting in "switch backs" like they do in the USA. When a track goes up or down, often it is straight up or straight down. When New Zealanders say a track is hard, you had better believe them!

Because of the underbrush and ferns hanging over it, the track was often invisible. But by following the orange markers, I was able to figure out where to put my boots. Then at about 10:30am, I lost the trail. I could no longer see markers! I looked around for signs of the track, but it was like being in the middle of a jungle (oh, for a GPS back then). From the lay of the land, I could work out where I thought the track went, so I did some pretty intense bush bashing as I climbed that hill. Finally, after fighting with ferns, roots, rocks and mud, I glimpsed another orange triangle and the track.

As the trail rose out of the valley, it started getting into sub-Alpine and then Alpine tundra. The environment changed from tall beech trees to alpine cabbage trees, and finally into tussocks and shrubs. Once the track was in the tussocks, it was marked by "snow poles": metal poles with orange triangles on them, or painted orange marks on top. Usually, when you stand at one marker, you can see the next one. But often, you have to hunt for it. Also, the trail is hard to follow between the tussocks. Even so, I think I prefer looking for the track in tussocks than in ferns. Finally, Lake Roe Hut came into sight, and I knew the climb and bush bashing had been worth it!

The Lake Roe Hut is surrounded by little lakes and alpine peaks. It is actually located at the Northern part of Lake Laffy, and the real Lake Roe is about a 20 minute walk from the hut. I stopped at the hut, unpacked my pack, and put my feet up for a well-earned rest.

After an hour or so, I walked over to see the actual Lake Roe. It was wonderful to hike around without a big pack on my back. I felt as light as air! As I came over the hill, I was greeted with such beauty. A small lake, but much larger than a "tarn", was surrounded by mountain peaks, large rock slabs, green snow grass, and brown tussocks. I felt privileged to be there. (Lake Angelus, my previous favorite high mountain lake, you have a contender!) A slight breeze made small waves on the lake and created a gentle lapping sound on the beach. I wanted to stay forever. But that breeze was also making me cold, so I made my way back to the hut.

It was a sweet little hut and once again, I had it all to myself. Because the Lake Roe Hut is in an alpine environment, I had a couple of keas come and entertain me whenever I went outside. A kea is a New Zealand parrot. They are the world's only wild alpine parrot, and are known to be one of the most intelligent birds. They are protected in New Zealand, and are a dark green color, but under their wing they have bright orange feathers. To survive in the harsh alpine environment, keas have become inquisitive, a characteristic which helps them find and utilize new food sources. Keas are endearing but mischievous, so I had to be careful not to leave any of my gear outside. However, they were beautiful and fun to watch. I could hear their claws as they walked across the peak of the hut. They would peer down into one window, walk to the other side, and then peer in that window. I knew they were hoping I would feed them, but that was strictly against the rules.

Rain had been forecast, so I spent the next day at the hut. The day was long, as I was still alone. While it stormed, I played solitaire and solo Farkle, and did lots of reading. Luckily, in most huts, there is a random selection of magazines. At about 5:00pm, I could see the weather starting to clear. I was feeling cooped up after being in the hut all day, so I hiked up to Lake Roe. Once again, I was rewarded by the beauty of the lake, this time with scattered clouds blowing over the mountain peaks.

The next day, Day Four, was clear and sunny. As I left the hut that morning, two of the keas came to wish me well, and to scold me for not leaving them any food! It was a perfect day to go across the top of the aptly named Pleasant Range. There was still some climbing to do, but after 36 hours of resting, I certainly felt renewed.

The trail wove its way across the tundra, going around lakes and tarns. I don't think I have ever seen so many tarns of all sizes, shapes and colors. I felt like I was on top of the world. I was! I was even enjoying the breeze, which would go through the tussocks and blow them like a wave. The sun sparkled on each ripple of the tarns, making them look like diamonds.

For my first hour of hiking, I could look back and see Lake Roe Hut. In the other direction, I could see all the way to the ocean and Dusky Sound. It looked very far away, but I thought, "That's where I am headed. Wow!"

According to my little map and description of the route, the trail would take me down to Loch Maree and my next hut. The trail came to the edge of the tops and I could see the Loch Maree below me. There were lots of roots, rocks, moss and slippery mud. It was an incredibly steep trail that went almost straight down. I had to go really slowly as I could have easily fallen and broken my neck in that type of stuff. NOT part of my plan! Often I had to turn around and face the mountain while I climbed down, as if I was on a ladder. The "hand holds" were the roots that your boots had been on just moments before, and most of it was slippery from the rains the day before. It took total concentration.

Occasionally, there was a chain to hold onto. I guess I was not the only one who thought it was steep. It took more than three hours to get down, certainly some of the hardest downwards hiking I had ever done. I was sure happy to be at the bottom.

There was a warning in the DoC brochure: *"Caution: If there has been continual rain it is recommended that you wait for more favorable conditions before completing this section, as the Seaforth River can be impassable due to flooding."* Luckily the Seaforth River was not flooding, but there was plenty of mud on the track. I had to be careful around muddy spots or I would sink down above my boots! Other than that, I had no problems getting to the Loch Maree Hut, arriving there about 4:00pm. Definitely another day to put my feet up.

While I was fixing my dinner, I heard voices. I had not seen a soul since I'd left Val at Lake Hauroko, so I was excited to be joined by Helen and Ian. They were sailing around the world, and as New Zealanders, they thought they'd sail around their own country first. After several weeks of their journey, they had anchored their boat in Dusky Sound. They then launched their kayaks to come as far as they could by river, and then hiked up to the hut. What an impressive journey to embark on - sailing around the world!

Helen and Ian wanted to hike to the tops the next day so they could see the views. I wanted to head out to Supper Cove on the Dusky Sound. So we went in different directions, knowing we would all be back in the hut that night. Before they started off, I warned them it was steep. REALLY steep!

Trail times to the Supper Cove Hut were listed as six to eight hours. As I wasn't carrying a heavy pack, I hoped it wouldn't take quite that long. But because I was going to the cove and back, I figured it might still be a long day. There were seven three-wire bridges to cross in order to get to Supper Cove. These were not the first three-wires I had gone over - the

Dusky has about 20 of them - but those seven bridges had to be crossed on the way back too! Without a full backpack, it was a lot easier to navigate them, but they certainly kept life interesting.

There was a rather large "slip" along the way. In New Zealand, a slip is a mudslide which obliterates the track. The thin soil, combined with steep hillsides and lots of rain, just slides off the mountain sides. Because the mud was so unstable, the track was re-routed to go above the slip, which added time and effort to my day.

I was blessed with another lovely day as I hiked along the river and out to Supper Cove. Even so, it took almost six hours to get to the water's edge. I knew I had another six hours to get back, so I decided not to go all the way to the Supper Cove Hut. When I was returning, I lost the track at the site of the slip. Bummer! I spent an hour bashing through the bush trying to find the trail. I finally found it but by the time I reached the hut, I had been hiking for over 12 hours. So much for my "easy" day!

When I got to the hut, Helen and Ian were already back from their climb to the tops. They agreed with me that it was a steep track, even by New Zealand standards. I assured them that I had seen their kayaks at the edge of the river, and they were high and dry and doing fine. After another night at the Lake Maree Hut, Ian and Helen headed back to their boat, and I went on towards the Kintail Hut. I still had three more days before I would finish the Dusky.

The day after Lake Maree mostly involved following a river along the valley floor. It was another fine day, so I felt very lucky. This was the section that could flood after a lot of rain, and the area Val impressed on me to be careful in. Fortunately, the river was down and I had no problems at all.

Since it was such a nice day, I took my time following the track. I spent hours going around mud bogs and then trying to find the trail. Sometimes

I just plowed right into the mud, occasionally sinking up to my knees. If I sank too deep, and pulled my leg out, there was the possibility my boot would come off. I really didn't want that to happen.

With me taking my time, enjoying the ferns, trees and mossy environment, it took all day to get to the Kintail Hut. I knew I wouldn't be going any further, so what would be the use of getting there too early? For all that, I didn't get to the hut until 6:30 that night! I realized I was enjoying myself, and doing a bit of lollygagging, but, good grief, I had taken three and a half hours longer than the suggested track time!

From the Kintail Hut, the track went to the Upper Spey Hut. It was not a long day distance wise, but the difficulty level was going to make it a long day in hours. The track climbed straight up again, crossing the top of Center Pass. Some of the trail was bare rock you had to scramble over; but thankfully, on the really steep and rough spots, there were chains to hold on to. There were lots of waterfalls along the way, and on top of the pass, it was spectacular once again.

Looking back from where I had come, I saw the most unusual little mountain called Tripod Hill. It looked just like a huge triangle plopped between the other mountains. My map showed that I had been next to Tripod Hill, but from below I couldn't make out the distinctive shape of the mountain. From the pass though, I could get the big picture, and was looking down on the triangular formation of Tripod Hill. I could also see the Seaforth River valley where I had been hiking for two days. It was impossible to see the trail since the bush was so lush, but looking down I could see the river snaking between the mountains. Once again, I felt like I was on top of the world – New Zealand passes do that to you.

While I was on the pass, I met two young men coming in from Lake Manapouri. One was from Scotland, the other from my old stomping ground of Cincinnati (where I was born and raised). It was just their second day out and they said it was already harder than they had expected. I told them they hadn't seen anything yet! They were only going to go in for one more day and then turn around and come out the way they went in. That was too bad because they would miss some of the most wonderful and interesting parts of the Dusky.

I stayed on the top of Center Pass for about an hour. It is unusual to be able to hang out on top of a pass, as it is usually too cold and windy. But it was warm and sunny that day, and I was totally enjoying it. It took another three hours to work my way down the steep trail to the Upper Spey Hut.

The last day was mostly downhill. I had some wire bridges to walk over, but I now felt pretty comfortable crossing them. And, as it was the last day of my trip, my pack was SO much lighter. But things are never as easy as they seem. As I headed out to the road, the Dusky had one last shot at me. I stepped into mud that went up over my boots. Oofta! "Dusky!" I shouted, "You just never give up do you?" But shortly thereafter, at 1:30pm, I got to the road and the sign that signaled the trail's end.

From there, it was a short hike to the Lake Manapouri power station and the boat dock. The boat wasn't scheduled to leave until 3:30pm, so I had time to wash mud off my boots and body, and fix myself a cup of tea and a second lunch.

While we were crossing Lake Manapouri, the captain's voice boomed over the loudspeaker:

"Would the lady who has just completed the Dusky please come up to the cabin."

Yikes! Was I in trouble?? It turned out he just wanted to meet me. I think he was impressed that I had done the Dusky on my own. It was great fun crossing the lake from the top deck with the captain. After the ride across Lake Manapouri, I made it back to my trusty van. I had survived another fun adventure. Who says you can't do the Dusky solo?

Lake Hauroko

Lake Roe

Access to Three Wire Bridge

Three Wire Bridge

Lots of Mud!

Contor Pass

Loch Maree

For more photos go to: http://still-going-strong.com

February 2006

Arthur's Pass

Situational awareness *or* **situation awareness** *(SA) is the perception of environmental elements with respect to time or space, the comprehension of their meaning, and the projection of their status after some variable has changed... Situation awareness involves being aware of what is happening in the vicinity, in order to understand how information, events, and one's own actions will impact goals and objectives, both immediately and in the near future.*

Wikipedia

The mountains around Arthur's Pass contain some very challenging terrain. The marked day walks in the park, all easily accessible from the Arthur's Pass village carparks, involve vertical ascents of around 1000 meters (3000 feet) and include several hours well above the tree line. The peaks are highly exposed to the weather, the tracks are often very steep (steep enough to require the walker to pull themselves up with their hands in some places) and are often marked only by poles strung across a rocky landscape. Below the tree line the bush is dense and thick. In common with many alpine areas the weather is subject to frequent and sudden change. There are frequent bluffs and cliffs and most creeks running down the mountains tumble over waterfalls in one place or another. Further, there are a number of harder routes within the park that require a high level of mountaineering skill and the use of ropes and other such equipment. In short, safely traversing the terrain requires at least a moderate level of experience, knowledge and equipment as it is true 'back country'.

Department of Conservation brochure

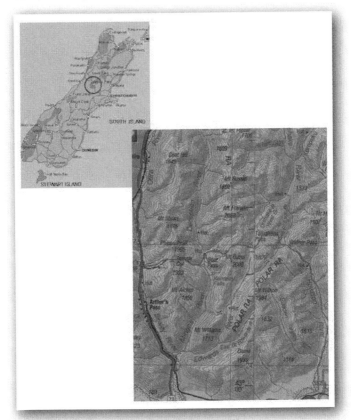

For more detail on maps, go to: http://still-going-strong.com

It all started in February of 2006 when I met Bill, a lovely DoC employee at the Arthur's Pass office. Bill helped me put together a trip that entailed four passes and joined five different valleys. He let me hire a map and copied pages from a couple of books that described the route because it wasn't shown on any maps. Does that sound like my kind of trip, or what?

I drove across the White Bridge just east of Arthur's Pass, and slept in my van at the Walker Pass trailhead. I awoke to a stunning red sunrise. Oops. "Red sky at night, shepherd's delight, Red sky in the morning, shepherds take warning" Well that saying came true in spades.

At 8:00am on Valentine's Day, I started up the Hawdon River, crossing it within the first few minutes, and multiple times over the next couple of hours. Then the rains came, and I was soon slogging through the mud. Bill had warned me that the Hawdon Hut had burned down the year before, so I could not expect to stay there. Sure enough when I got to the Hawdon Hut, all that was left was the "long drop" (that's Kiwi for Outhouse). A brief thought passed through my brain that I could stay dry in there but, ick...no way! "Roughing it" does have its limits! So I went on up the track. There was not much in the way of comfortable flat ground. I wanted to set up my homemade tarp to cook and sit under, so it would be best in the trees where I could tie it up. I found a reasonably soft, semi-flat place below Walker Pass. It was pretty wet and not terrific, but I figured it would work ok for one rainy afternoon and evening.

The next morning started off rather foggy but the track was mostly through trees and bush. By the time I reached the top of the pass, it had turned into a beautiful day. Over Walker Pass, it was back into the bush and to the bottom of the valley. There wasn't much of a trail, but my description told me to follow a small stream up to Tarn Col (my second pass). It was pretty steep but I was getting used to this type of travel. I used my hands and arms to do a lot of climbing. I was well rewarded when I crested the ridge and found a little saddle with a tarn in the middle of it. How unusual to have a tarn basically on a ridge top. No wonder it is called: Tarn Col!

From the col, I looked down into Tarahuna Pass. The description said a trail led to the pass, but I couldn't find it. Maybe now, in hindsight, I should have looked harder. I tried the stream bed, but it cliffed out and was quite terrifying, so I went back up to the col. I chose the scree slope to the left of where I was. It was "hard pan" dirt, with lots of hanging rocks above it. Pretty scary but still better than the cliffs, and besides, I had to get down somehow.

I gingerly worked my way out till I found myself plastered face-in, up against a very steep, hardpan dirt slope, inching my way down. I only had about four body lengths to get down, but one slip here and I would fall the rest of the way, leaving behind lots of skin in the process. I dug my fingers into the side of the hill as my boots reached out for any purchase they could find: a small clump of grass, a small stone sticking out (oops, that one came loose), or a bump of dirt. Slowly I negotiated inch by inch until I could turn around and actually walk down the still steep slope.

Tarahuna Pass is an interesting place. It is next to a mountain that totally collapsed during an earthquake in 1929. They call it Falling Mountain. How original! The pass was just a jumble of rocks and boulders, a large part of which are remains of Falling Mountain. But, luckily, there was a small spring on the slope I had just come down, and I was able to find, once again, a fairly flat and comfortable spot to camp out. I could see up to where I would go tomorrow. It was going to be another early morning climb. Nothing new about that!

When I woke the next morning, it was totally socked in. Because I had been out for four days on this trip, I was not sure what the latest weather predictions were. I hung out at my camp, reading and drinking tea, waiting to see what the clouds would do. I did not think it would be a good idea to climb the next ridge if it was raining. It was hard enough in good weather! So I waited, and waited, and waited... (I'm not very good at this "waiting" stuff). There were a couple of keas to entertain me, but knowing how destructive they could be, I had to shoo them away before they got too close to my gear. Finally, at about 10:00am, with the clouds still pretty thick, I decided to change my route and hike down the Edwards drainage to the road. But, I thought, before I do that, I'd hike just a little higher to see what it was like. As I started up the steep slope, the clouds cleared and next thing I knew I was under blue skies once again. I was sure glad I hadn't headed back down already!

This part of the route didn't have a name, but I could see a little spot of snow up the hill and the pass just above that. As I climbed up, I came to another high mountain tarn. I climbed past the tarn and noticed there were two ways up. One was the more direct route just above my head, while the other seemed to be a trail that zigzagged up to the right. I chose the more direct route, and up I went, right next to the snow I had seen from Tarn Col. By 2:30pm, I was on top of my fourth pass, once again looking over mountain peaks in every direction. I could even see Tarn Col in the distance. I was also looking down into Lake Mavis, which was a magnificent sight. Three sides were steep mountain scree slopes, and one side of the lake fell into the valley toward Goat Pass. The sunlight sparkled on top of the lake like thousands of tiny diamonds. Wow! I felt so happy to be there!

Working my way down to Lake Mavis was a lot more fun than my trip down to Tarahuna Pass. It was soft scree, and every step was like walking in pudding. It made the scree in a four-foot radius slide with me. Like an astronaut on the moon, I took giant leaps and bounds, sinking into the scree and basically running down the hill. It was so much fun, I was tempted to go back up and do it again. "Whoa Talie, we still have a long way to go!" So I took my time wandering around the edge of Lake Mavis till I found the perfect camping spot. After my last two nights in marginal spots, this was ideal. The sun was still shining strong, so I had plenty of time to take a dip in the lake.

Before dinner, I hiked over to look down on Goat Pass. This is part of the route they use in the famous "Coast to Coast" race, an endurance event consisting of running, biking and kayaking. The contestants start on the West Coast near Greymouth and race all the way to the ocean just south of Christchurch on the East Coast. It is a pretty intense race, even for the fittest of athletes!

From my little perch looking over Goat Pass, I could see my day's next route – my final pass called Temple Col. Oh dear. It looked really gnarly! What was I thinking? I really didn't know if I should tackle that on my own. I tried to remind myself, yet again, that passes usually look worse than they actually turn out to be. I'd make that decision tomorrow. Right now, it was time to fix my pasta and a cup of tea, before a night's rest.

The next morning, I was greeted by more blue skies. But when I looked down into the valley of the Goat Pass, I saw it was totally filled with clouds. So, that was what I had been dealing with yesterday morning when I awoke in the valley in the clouds! It is just low-lying fog that settles in the passes.

I could still see very clearly – maybe too clearly – Temple Col. It looked jagged and rocky, and I didn't like that sight one little bit. "Well," I said, "Let's have another cup of tea." It was so warm and sunny, I decided to spend more time enjoying this gorgeous spot. I sunbathed, read, had another little dip in the water ("Ooh, that is C-C-COLD"), and lazed around my campsite.

While I was relaxing, I pondered my next move. I thought it prudent to take Temple Col off the itinerary. I decided to just go down to the hut at Goat Pass and spend the night there, before hiking out to the road. Temple Col had scared me enough to make me change my route.

At about 2:00pm, I finally started away from the lake. I realized it would only take an hour to get to Goat Pass Hut, so why rush? I would rather spend time up here by this beautiful lake than down there in the hut. So, after about 50 steps, I took off my pack, boots and socks, and put my feet back in the water! At that moment, I heard voices. I looked up and saw people coming over the same ridge that I had come over the day before. It looked like they had taken the upwards route I didn't take, and I wondered what their route was like? So I decided to wait until they got to the lake and ask them.

Sure enough, four lovely Kiwis showed up. Believe it or not, they were about my age. ("Gray Hares" as we would refer to them in Crested Butte - skiers, hikers, bikers, soft-ballers, etc. of "a certain age"). These hikers were "gray hares" for sure! How awesome was that? So Brian, Peter, Margo and Selwyn and I started talking. On comparing notes of our routes over this last saddle, it seemed like mine was steeper on both sides, while theirs was not so steep but a bit longer.

I mentioned that I had planned to go over Temple Col, but it looked too rugged for me to do solo. Did I really hear them say, "We're quite keen on going over Temple Col ourselves."? And did I really ask if I could accompany them? And was their answer, "Yes, of course!"? Now, I do believe in angels, and these were my "Kiwi Angels". They got here at the perfect time. They were going to camp the night at Lake Mavis, and I didn't want to spoil their experience of this beautiful lake. So I told them I would go down to Goat Pass Hut and meet them in the morning when they came down on their way to Temple Col.

As planned, I met up with them the next morning, and we worked our way up the side of the hill toward Temple Col. It turned out that the worst part of this section of the track was getting to the pass. There was no real trail and we worked our way along the side of a gully. It was steep "side hill" walking, going in and out of steep gullies filled with scree. It took a long time just to get to the end of the valley where the climb to the pass would even start.

Shortly after we started the climb, we took our lunch stop. We found some tussocks, but it was so steep we needed to be sure our packs didn't roll off. Everyone pulled their wet laundry out of their packs to dry on the grass. We looked like a yard sale ready to happen!

Needless to say, as is my experience, the pass was not nearly as gnarly as I thought it would be. It was steep and rocky and took some navigation, but it was just a giant boulder field, very similar to climbing a mountain in Colorado. I was so glad I didn't go down from Goat Pass and miss this final part of my planned trip.

We took lots of photos at the top. We were looking directly across Arthur's Pass at Mt. Rolleston and the surrounding mountains. Back the way that we had come, we could see the Goat Pass Trail and Lake Mavis above it. There was still plenty of snow on the peaks, and they were jagged and beautiful. It was unusual to have someone with me who could take my photo - usually I had to set a timer and run round in front of the camera. But now, I had photos of me looking every which way!

From the pass we hiked down into the Temple Col ski area. It was not as steep or rugged as the other side, but it was still loose scree and we had to be careful. There was a hut at the ski area called the Page Shelter. Unfortunately the bedrooms were locked, as was the long drop. But we were out of the wind and cold, we could cook our dinner inside, and even "camp out" in the main room.

The next day, I said good-bye to my angels and hiked the rest of the way down to the Arthur's Pass road. I had to hitchhike out to where I had left my van just past White Bridge. Then I stopped in the store at Arthur's Pass for juice and cookies for my favorite DoC workers. Who did I see in the store? My Kiwi angels. One of them needed to get to Christchurch to fly home to see an old friend, so I agreed to drive him there that afternoon. They invited me over for a shower first! Then it was on to Christchurch, where I dropped him off and then I went to visit with my friends who live in Lincoln.

Dancing with Wild Spaniard

Looking towards my next pass!

Looking Back on Tarn Col

Kea going after my hiking poles

Looking Down on Lake Mavis

On Top of Temple Col

For more photos go to: http://still-going-strong.com

March 2006

The Dragon's Teeth

The clearest way into the Universe is through a forest wilderness.

John Muir

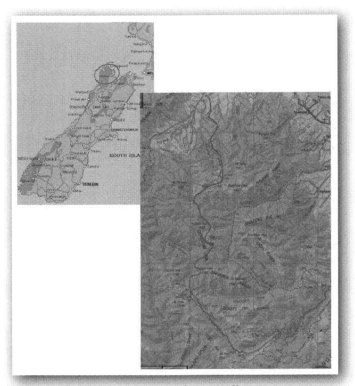

For more detail on maps, go to: http://still-going-strong.com

The Dragons Teeth route links the Aorere and Cobb Valleys in Golden Bay. It is unmarked and suitable for trampers with a high degree of fitness and off-track experience. You should allow at least five days and, if possible, one or two extra days to complete this trip. Streams and rivers are not bridged and the route has many exposed sections.

"Stretching between the Cobb Valley in the south and the Aorere Valley in the north, the range is one of contrasts: delicate tarns fringed by bogs where sundews trap hapless insects; peaks so precipitous they cast shadows even at noon in summer; stunted beech forest mingling with rocky outcrops; the jumbled chaos of the Lead Hills, where granite blocks lie like some sort of precarious game.

Much of the Douglas range offers challenging tramping. Its most rugged section around the Dragon's Teeth is not for the faint-hearted, but the satisfaction of traversing the range is measurably all the greater for it.

Department of Conservation brochure

Back in December, before the Three Tarns Hikes and Dusky, I hiked into the Kahurangi National Forest to a hut at Boulder Lake. It was my first hike of the season, a supposedly eight-hour hike that actually took me nine hours. (In New Zealand, at the start of a track, it tells you how long it should take to get to the next hut. But I wonder who decides the durations on these trails? A little old lady like me? Or some big strong rugby player?!) On that trip, I spent two nights at the Boulder Lake Hut all by myself and explored the valley and lake while I was there.

One of my favorite pastimes when I am in a hut by myself, is to read the "hut book". This is a logbook, placed in huts by the Department of Conservation. When you get to a hut, you are supposed to sign in and write down when you arrive, when you are leaving, and what your destination is. That way, if someone gets lost, the Search and Rescue people can check the hut books and see if the lost party had been there. It is a good system, and I think most people sign in.

The most entertaining parts of the hut books are comments about the trail, the hut and, sometimes, stories or poems. Yes, people can get pretty bored in a backcountry hut! In the Boulder Lake Hut book, I noticed several entries about coming in from Green Saddle and doing a trail known as

"The Dragon's Teeth." Wow, my little brain piped up: "Dragon's Teeth. That sounds interesting!" I looked on my map and saw the route they had taken. It looked like fun! But that would have to be another time because I didn't have enough food with me to take on a six-day hike. Another idea for the "back burner".

Let's fast forward a couple of months to the end of my Kiwi season. It was March 2006, and I decided to finish my hiking in New Zealand by doing "The Dragon's Teeth" route. I drove back to the little town of Takaka, and parked my van at the end of the route. I had arranged for a shuttle to take me to the start of the trek. My shuttle driver, a local dentist, took me to the Trilobite Hut, just past Cobb Reservoir. This entailed about two hours of driving up a gravel road that was only one lane in some places. It's not only the tracks that are exciting around here. Driving the roads can be a thrill as well!

I spent the night at the Trilobite Hut and the next morning hiked up the Cobb Valley. This was a relatively mellow start to my trip. The track followed the valley floor of the Cobb River with a slow gentle rise. Then I headed uphill until I reached the Fenella Hut mid-afternoon. The Fenella Hut is named after Fenella Druce, one of four people killed when a hut in Mt. Cook National Park was blown off its site. One of the hut's best features was the stain glass window in the "long drop". Yet another "loo with a view"! There was even a hand basin made out of rocks, complete with cold running water.

The track up to Fenella Hut was a normal DoC track, but after the hut, the "track" became a "route", which may or may not have markings on it. I knew I was stretching myself so I thought: "Ok, Talie. There is always an option of turning back."

The route went along a ridge, going around jagged peaks and through little passes. It was a scenic spot, but definitely "out there", and "up there". Even though it was pretty rugged, there was a path of sorts. I occasionally saw a pole, and there were cairns here and there. This was before the advent of personal GPS devices, but I did have a map, and I never felt that I didn't know where I was going. At the top of the ridge, I got a view of the Dragons Teeth - very impressive steep peaks at the end of the valley.

Before I got to the next hut, the Lonely Lake Hut, I could see Lonely Lake across a very deep valley. It was aptly named. At least I knew where I was going, even if it looked a little daunting to get there. I had to avoid some shear rock faces, and I would have to go all the way down the valley, across the stream, and up the other side. I had a bit of a hike still in front of me.

Lonely Lake is in a small basin surrounded by bluffs. The hut, built by the Golden Bay Alpine and Tramping Club in 1973, was small and rather tired. If it had been snowing or pouring with rain, I'd have stayed in it if I really had to. But I had my tarp with me, and it was a still, clear evening, so I found a perfect spot to camp by the lake. Tobi and Christina, a Swiss couple I had met at the Fenella Hut, came by my camping spot, had a quick swim in the lake, and then headed on up the next hill. That was ok with me because I was reveling in the solitude where I was.

The next morning, I climbed up to a rock formation called the Drunken Sailors. I met up with Tobi and Christina and we decided to go to the Adelaide Tarn Hut together. This promised to be a rough section of the route and it was good to be with someone. My angels had once again sent me companions when I needed them. Tobi and Christina were part of the mountain rescue group in the Swiss town they came from, and as I had been on Crested Butte Search and Rescue for many years, we had lots of stories and common interests.

We hiked under the Drunken Sailors, and bashed around a while, trying, and failing, to find the trail down. Fortunately, even though it was steep, the bush wasn't too thick, so we just headed down. We went from holding one tree to the next, hand over hand until we reached the bottom. The Anatoki River, which flowed through the valley floor, didn't have a bridge, but it was not deep and we waded across.

We could see where we needed to climb the next ridge, so we kept looking for the track that would lead us up there. We didn't find any markings or track, so we just started climbing. We found a bit of a trail, but I think we missed the real route because, before I knew it, I was hanging onto the side of the mountain by my fingernails! It was pretty scary. Tobi and Christina were doing the same thing. It was very slow going but, just when I thought my arms would give out, we got up into the tussocks. Right in front of us were the jagged mountain peaks called the Dragon's Teeth.

Crossing the saddle at the top, we could see the Adelaide Tarn Hut. It reminded me of the old Lonely Lake Hut. Built in 1963, it would be welcomed in a storm. But yet again, as the weather was so good, I decided to camp out. My new friends, Tobi and Christina, camped on the other side of the lake so we did enjoy a bit of solitude. And, having done the hardest part of the route together, we knew we would probably hike separately for the rest of the trip. I was happy they had shown up in my life at the perfect time!

I was a little concerned the next day because my map showed me going through a saddle called The Eye of the Needle. It all sounded a bit daunting, but it turned out to be just a small pass between two very tall rock formations.

I had seen all these formations on my map - Drunken Sailors, Dragon's Teeth, Eye of the Needle - but it was always fun seeing the actual rocks and why they were so named.

The trail then went down the ridge, following a few scattered cairns till I was at Green Saddle. There I could look down and see Boulder Lake and the hut next to it. I headed down and across the valley, which was full of shoulder-high tussocks. It was impossible to see any sort of track among the tussocks, and parts of the valley floor were rather soggy, but I finally made it. Back at Boulder Lake Hut! To confirm it, there in the hut book was my entry from a couple of months before!

After camping for the last two nights, I definitely appreciated a comfortable hut. The next day, it was a bit of a hike to get up to the Brown Cow saddle. This was my third time on this section of track, so I felt I knew it fairly well, even if I never seemed to do it any faster! Some rock crevasses along the trail always got my attention. When I looked into them, it was impossible to see how deep they were. I wouldn't want to be doing this track after the sun had gone down!

Tobi and Christina decided to hike out with me. I had told them my van was parked at the trailhead, so I could give them a ride back into town. Oh, it was so nice to have my lovely little van parked at the end of a track. It was well worth the extra hour of transport in the beginning!

Trail along the ridge tops

Lonely Lake

The Dragons Teeth

Adelaide Tarn

Coming across the tops

Looking down on Boulder Lake from Green Saddle

For more photos go to: http://still-going-strong.com

Antarctica

● ● ●

I can complain because rose bushes have thorns, or rejoice
because thorn bushes have roses. It's all how you look at it.

J. Morley

MOST OF MY STORIES IN this book are about solo backpacking trips, but as I get so many questions about my 14 months in Antarctica, I thought I would include a chapter about this astounding white continent - and this adventure also happened during my 60's.

Why Antarctica? During my two winters in Alaska back in 1990-92, I had lots of time to read. Some of the books were written by people who had experienced a polar winter. By polar winter, I mean a winter where the sun doesn't rise for several months. The descriptions of the "sun coming back" and the colors and feelings of elation fascinated me. I put polar winter on my "to do list", never dreaming that I would be going south to Antarctica rather than north to the Arctic!

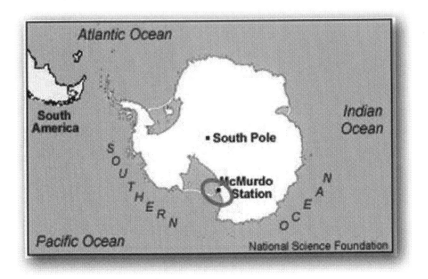

NOVEMBER 2007

NOT SO ALONE ON THE ICE

MCMURDO STATION IS AN ANTARCTIC research center on the south tip of Ross Island. The island is located in the New Zealand-claimed Ross Dependency on the shore of McMurdo Sound. McMurdo is operated through the United States Antarctic Program, a branch of the National Science Foundation. The station is the largest community in Antarctica, capable of supporting up to 1,258 residents. All personnel and cargo going to or coming from Amundsen–Scott South Pole Station first pass through McMurdo.

It all started in the spring of 2007, when a friend suggested I might want to go to McMurdo Station in Antarctica. I was intrigued by the idea. I put together my résumé, applied on line, went to a job fair, and then had a couple of phone interviews. Next thing I knew, I had been offered a job at McMurdo. As a janitor! Well, I'm really good at tidying, and I have been cleaning toilets my whole life, but no one had ever paid me for it....until now!

First, I had to pass a battery of physical exams. I don't think I have ever been checked over so thoroughly! Then some orientation meetings. Come on, guys...how much about "janitor" do I really need to know? And then long flights from Denver to LAX, LAX to Sydney, and Sydney to Christchurch, home of the U.S Antarctic Program Center.

At the center, they outfitted me with all the CWC (cold weather clothing) I would need to stay warm on the ice:

2 x sets of long johns
4 x pairs of socks
2 x work pants
2 x work shirts
1 x fleece jacket
2 x fleece pants
1 x pair wind pants
4 x mitten/gloves
3 x hats
1 x pair boots
1 x neck gaiter
1 x sunglasses
1 x giant down jacket called "Big Red"!

I was ready for the frozen continent!

After a five hour flight from Christchurch, our C140 plane touched down on the ice runway. Yes, you read it right...ice runway! Even though it was -20 degree (F) weather, with a 10 knot wind, it was incredibly beautiful. The sun, which had risen for the first time the day before, was setting and the colors were amazing. The whole environment was white and glowing with pink and orange from the sky. That sunset lasted for five hours, even though the sun that day had only been up for one hour.

Was I really standing on the sea ice in Antarctica!? Was I upside down on the bottom of the planet and not falling off? It was hard to believe. I wasn't even cold, thanks to my CWC. Actually, I looked like a Pillsbury Dough Boy. I kept thinking, "I'm in Antarctica! ANTARCTICA!!! This is so unreal."

We walked on a hard-packed snow surface and then I realized I was standing above the ocean. I guess if the ice could support the weight of the plane, I wasn't going to fall through. It was at least a mile thick! Everything was pristine white with majestic mountains in the distance.

I WAS IN ANTARCTICA!

My brain was having a hard time wrapping itself around that fact. I really *was* in Antarctica…

Since this was a job, and not a holiday, we had plenty to do. The ice runway was a 20 minute drive from McMurdo. Then, more orientation meetings, room assignments, linen packets to pick up (I became very familiar with those packets later in my ice time), luggage to retrieve, and dormitories and rooms to find. I felt totally bombarded with emotions, visuals, and realizations. Looking out my dorm window towards a glorious sunset further reminded where I actually was! And I even had a big laugh about sleeping in the <u>same</u> bed for six months - a huge change from my regular lifestyle.

The very next day we were on the job from 7:30am until 5:30pm. My work became pretty routine. It doesn't matter where you are, cleaning is cleaning. I had been promoted to lead janitor which meant I was in charge of a team. In October, when all the other workers showed up, I switched to night shift. After all, when it is 24 hour sunlight, what is night?

Life is not all about working. Even in Antarctica, where I worked six days a week, nine hours a day, I still found some time to "recreate"! During the summer, if you were lucky, you could attend "Happy Camper School." This was training for the scientists and their helpers who worked away from base and out on the ice. It covered what to do in an emergency, and how to set up a camp if needed. I was pretty excited when I found out I could do Happy Camper too. It was a good thing too, because I would need that knowledge later that winter.

After a bit of discussion about the dangers of the ice, we learned how to set up the tents, how to build a quinzhee (a sort of sunken igloo), how to build a snow wall, and how to set up and use an outdoor kitchen on the ice (including how to melt water). You're right...I was in my element!

One of the biggest problems, along with the cold out on the ice, is wind. Needless to say, the wind can lower your temperature dramatically. So they would teach us ways of getting out of the wind. The most-used method was to build a snow wall. All of the emergency kits had a shovel and saw. The saw was to cut blocks of ice and then we pried them out with the shovel. And, just like in kindergarten, we built a wall.

Digging down into the ice and creating a snow pit was another way to get out of the wind. So when we had the choice of sleeping in a tent, building a quinzhee, being surrounded by a snow wall, or digging a snow pit, I chose the snow pit option.

I dug down about five feet and lined the bottom with sleeping pads and a couple of sleeping bags. I cut cubby holes in the sides to put my book, water, and other items. I had quite the cozy space to sleep in! I even used one of the sleds to pull over the top to cut out some of the light. I loved Happy Camper School!

During my time on the ice, I also volunteered as a librarian. All of the dormitories had an extensive collection of paperbacks that people had brought with them and left behind, or ordered while they were there. The station also had its own library with a decent selection of hardback books. A lot were on Antarctic subjects: exploration to the South Pole, Shackleton, Scott etc. But there was also a good range of fiction and non-fiction books; it was nice to read about something other than Antarctica from time to time!

In December, I heard a winter position would be available. It would still be a lead janitor position, but the work involved doing laundry. When everyone arrives in Antarctica, they are issued a linen packet. This packet contains a mattress pad, two sheets and a pillowcase, a blanket, and a duvet (or comforter). While you are in Antarctica, it is your responsibility to wash your own linens. But when you get ready to go home, you put your dirty linens in a plastic bag and send it to the laundry.

One person had seven months over winter (February till August) to wash, dry and fold that linen. That meant 2400 sheets, 1200 pillowcases, 1200 mattress pads, 1200 blankets and 1200 duvets all needed to be washed, dried, folded and put in plastic bags. I thought it sounded like a great job for me!

I called my sons and said, "I think I am staying for winter. But I have to pass a psych-exam first." Craig replied, "Mom, don't they KNOW you are crazy if you want to spend the winter in Antarctica?!" Steve said, "Mom, don't come back and then wish you had stayed!"

Believe it or not, I did pass those psych-exams and got the winter position. It was quite an emotional feeling in April when the last plane left for

New Zealand, knowing we wouldn't see another one till August. Part of those emotions was the excitement of seeing the summer crew leave and realizing it was just the winter crew now. While another part of it was knowing that I was about as isolated as I could possibly be and still be on Planet Earth!

One of the really nice things about staying for winter was that I got my own room. No roommate to deal with – not that my roommate wasn't fine. It was just nice to have my "own" place. Another plus was that I was in charge of housing for the winter, so I could choose the perfect room! It was on the third floor with a great view over the ice. Actually, most of the time, it was too dark to get a view, but I liked the idea of having to go up three flights of stairs every time I went to my room. I needed the exercise!

Of course the gym was still open, and since I was back to working days, I started getting up at 5:30am and going to the gym at 6:00am. Then I could get back to my room and shower and be ready to start work at 7:30am.

Ok, I was supposed to be "roughing it" down here in Antarctica. Right? When I think of the winters in Alaska, where we had to start a fire in the wood stove to get warm, cook on propane, use an outhouse, run a generator, and do our laundry by hand in a tin tub, I really can't say I roughed it in Antarctica. There was a full on electricity plant, flushing toilets, washing machines and dryers, three square meals a day, and the lights worked by flipping a switch!

I became good friends with two other ladies who liked to hike: Annie at McMurdo and Therese at Scott Base, the New Zealand-operated facility. We would have brunch together on Sundays, then go for a hike. If we were going off base, we had to sign out at the fire hall. We had to let them know where we were planning to go, how long we would be gone, and we had to take a radio with us. After our hike, we had to check back in with the fire hall. It was a bit of a hassle, but you didn't want to wander off and get stranded somewhere in Antarctica during the winter.

Going for a hike always felt like an adventure. We used head lamps and were usually gone for three to four hours. We couldn't go very far during the winter months, or even the summer months for that matter. By that time, I knew most of the trails by heart. It was just good to be doing something physical that didn't involve work, or the gym. Annie and Therese felt exactly the same.

Since I had experience with Search and Rescue in Crested Butte, I was also able to join the Winter Search and Rescue Team. This team was made up of people from Scott Base and McMurdo. We trained all day Thursday, every other week. Being able to "go play" in the cold and snow was something I really looked forward to.

Before winter started though, I had a request from a school in Japan. One of the classes took on a project to get a photo of a little Japanese doll, called a Tengu, on all 7 continents. A Tengu is a type of legendary creature found in Japanese folk lore. They asked, if they sent me a Tengu, would I take a photo of it in Antarctica and email it to them. Thus, before the last planes took off, I received a package from Japan with a 2 cute little Tengus. (I left the pottery Tengu in Antarctica, but the little stuffed Tengu still travels with me when I go backpacking.)

APRIL 2008

An Unplanned Adventure
There was one winter adventure that was more than I had bargained for. It happened during April, so it was not totally dark yet.

There had been a problem out on the sea ice. A couple of bulldozers had fallen through some melt ice. On the huge ice sheets during the summer months, some of the ice on the top melts and forms little lakes. Then, when it turns colder, those little lakes start to freeze and a thin layer of ice forms on the top of them. During this time of year, you have to be especially careful not to take a piece of heavy equipment over the thin ice. Whoops, that was just what had happened.

Because there were lots of people trying to get the bulldozers out of the water (they wouldn't have sunk because there was still solid ice beneath the melt ponds), the station manager asked Search and Rescue to go to the scene and take extra survival equipment, in case someone was hurt. Some of the team went in trucks to be on the scene early, while I joined the team leader, Kish, in a Hagglund all-terrain carrier with the extra survival gear.

While Kish and I were headed to the scene, a "Condition 1" storm came up. Condition 1 represents the worst weather conditions, and can involve wind speeds greater than 55 knots (63 mph), wind chills colder than minus 100F, or visibility of less than 100 feet. Thankfully, poles marked our route across the ice. We knew we had to follow from pole to pole if the visibility was low, which was often the case in a storm or in the darkness.

Kish and I were following the marked route, but then we lost the marker poles. I had a GPS to direct us, but we found out later that it had not been updated with the correct information. So, as I was telling him which way the "road" was...or where I thought it was...

WHAM!!

The next thing we knew the Hagglund had fallen on its side. All of a sudden, bells and whistles started going off...it was like we were in a disco in hell.

Beep! Flash! Beep! Flash! BEEP!! FLASH!!

Kish was on top of me, and I was squashed between him and my door that was now resting on the ice. It was noisy and confusing.

Beep! Flash! Beep! Flash! BEEP!! FLASH!!

Kish asked if I was ok. I said yes. Was he ok? Above the beep, beep, beeps, I heard him say he was.

The Hagglund engine was revving itself, and everything was still going crazy.

BEEP!! FLASH!!

BEEP!! FLASH!!

BEEP!! FLASH!!

Neither of us knew exactly why we had crashed, or what was on the outside. We didn't know if we were in water, or in a more stable situation. The wind was howling outside, it was dark and it was cold. We had no choice but to turn the engine off.

Once we turned off the Hagglund, we assessed our situation. Luckily, we had not fallen in water, but we had been driving on an ice cornice and it had collapsed, flipping us on our side and dropping us down about five feet. We radioed to the base to tell them we were stuck. The dispatcher contacted the rescue crew, who were coming back from the bulldozer site, and gave them our co-ordinates. Unfortunately, they couldn't get to us and, because of the storm, they never even saw us.

The head of McMurdo station came on the radio and asked, "Are you prepared to spend the night out there?"

Kish looked at me and I looked at him, and we both said – "I'm ok with it." So Kish replied that we were prepared to wait on the ice until morning. What was a Condition 1 storm between friends??

At that point, we had decisions to make. Should we spend the night in the Hagglund or put up a tent on the ice? We still weren't sure why we had fallen on our side, and didn't know if the Hagglund was resting in a safe place. We were also concerned that being surrounded by metal during an Antarctic winter night might not be a good thing! Kish ventured out and reported that we should set up a camp on the ice.

In a situation like that, it was important to get to work. Both Kish and I had done the Happy Camper training. We knew what we had to do.

First, build a snow wall. The storm was abating and we could start building straight away. Our survival bag contained a saw, so we cut snow blocks and made our wall.

We then set up one of the tents next to the wall, where it was more protected. We had warm sleeping bags and pads to protect us from the cold ground, and a stove to melt snow and ice for water.

Just as we were about to dive into our tent, the wind changed directions. We now needed wind protection on the other side! Kish was nice enough to say he would build that wall, and I could go ahead and get into the tent. He joined me after putting up more snow blocks.

We were safe and protected in our little tent but, I have to admit, I didn't get much sleep. Kish didn't either. During the accident, the adrenaline rush of fear and survival had possibly depleted my body of potassium. I also think I was so focused on building our shelter that I let myself get dehydrated, so when I lay in my sleeping bag, my legs started cramping. I was in excruciating pain, and the only way to get rid of cramps like that was to stand up. It was a long night...

It was great when it got light, but there wasn't much warmth from the sun. Kish and I tried to walk around as much as possible to keep our hands and feet warm. I was pretty uncomfortable but I was fairly sure that I didn't have frostbite, or frostnip.

We were glad to see Search and Rescue approaching the next morning, even if it did take until 11:30am for them to reach us. Oh dear… Search and Rescue people rescuing other Search and Rescue people. How embarrassing!

JUNE 2008

SURVIVING THE MID-WINTER POLAR PLUNGE
As you've read, I do not like to jump in cold water. But as this might be the only time I would experience a polar winter, I knew I'd "go for it" when the time came for the infamous mid-winter Polar Plunge!

Near the water intake for Scott Base, there was an area where the ice was cleared down to the sea-water. This was salty ocean water, with a freezing temperature of 28 degrees Fahrenheit. Take it from me…that is COLD! I'd heard the powers that be at McMurdo had forbidden a polar plunge there, so those of us who were certifiably crazy enough to do this, went over to Scott Base. Those Kiwis were just as mad as we were!

I could have done a skinny dip, but ended up borrowing a bathing suit. I wasn't THAT crazy! Then, I put on a belt. The belt would be attached to a rope in case they had to pull me out. I wrapped up in a blanket and rushed out to the "pool". When it was my turn, I dropped my blanket, and….

1, 2, 3….JUMP!

Boy, oh boy… that was the coldest I had ever been! I went totally under the water and it took my breath away. I then climbed the ladder as fast as I could and wrapped back up in my blanket. The clever Kiwis at Scott Base had rigged up a kind of hot tub, so I jumped straight into that. It was quite the adventure, albeit a freezing one, but at least I could say:

"I d-d-d-d-d-did it!"

Now, whenever there is a challenge to jump into cold water, I decline. I have done the ultimate cold water plunge. I don't have to do it anymore!

AUGUST 2008

HERE COMES THE SUN
The route of the sun is fascinating when you experience a polar winter. During the summer months, the sun goes around in a circle in the sky, and never sets. At McMurdo, it first set for a few minutes about February 20. Then it set for longer and longer each day until it finally set for good around April 20. Even though the sun didn't come above the horizon, during the rest of April and half of May, there was a period of "dusky light". This was similar to the hour before sunrise or after sunset.

Towards the end of May, the light got less and less until it became dark for all of June and most of July. At the end of July, if I went outside the station where I could see the northern horizon, there was a bright red strip of light just on the horizon. Very exciting! Then, a little bit of dusky light would show up and it would stay light for longer and longer each day.

The dark phase of winter also had its own beauty. The moon (in whatever stage it was in) would go in a circle in the sky (like the sun did in the summer). And when the Australis Borealis was going off – it was amazing!

The last few weeks before the sun came back, I witnessed an interesting phenomenon. The sun was still below the horizon and the Antarctic air was still very cold. This created very colorful clouds, known as Nacreous clouds. They were some of the most interesting and beautiful clouds I had ever seen:

*Nacreous clouds, sometimes called **mother-of-pearl** clouds, are rare but once seen are never forgotten. They are mostly visible within two hours after sunset or before dawn when they blaze unbelievably bright with vivid and slowly shifting iridescent colors. They are filmy sheets slowly curling and uncurling, stretching and contracting in the semi-dark sky. Compared with dark scudding low altitude clouds that might be present, nacreous clouds stand majestically in almost the same place - an indicator of their great height.*

www.atoptics.co.uk

I had wanted to do a polar winter because I had read about the experience of the light coming back and seeing the sun after such a long absence. We could see the sun shining on the mountains across the Ross Ice Shelf, but the sun hadn't hit McMurdo yet. So I went with one of the researchers and we drove to a higher spot. And there, coming up just above the horizon and through the ice fog was the SUN! I can't explain how incredible it was to get a glimpse of that beautiful ball of fire. I felt like it was life changing. My whole body rejoiced in the light.

That first day, the whole sun doesn't even come above the horizon – only a portion of it for a few minutes. It actually takes three days for the full sun to come into view. And then after just two months, it is up for 24 hours.

OCTOBER 2008

TIME TO LEAVE THE ICE

Our skeleton staff on the ice would soon be joined by dozens of other scientists and associated workers. We had gotten pretty spoiled with only 250 people on the station. All of a sudden there were 500 people – people that were not part of our "winter family". It was mentally difficult to deal with the population doubling, so when my time to leave came around, I was more than ready to go. Before I left, I trained my replacement in the laundry. Those machines, with all their idiosyncrasies, had become my friends and they needed proper treatment!

I was all geared up and packed, but I had an extra couple of days to cool my heels (pun intended!), because the planes couldn't get in. Finally, on October 8, 2008, I boarded a C17 bound for New Zealand.

To this day, I feel blessed to have experienced Antarctica. Many of the friends I made down there still go year after year. But for me, another winter there would have meant missing the Crested Butte summer....and I love Crested Butte summers!

For more photos go to: http://still-going-strong.com

Tasmania

• • •

The process of daily living is often intense and whimsical. The joy of it, and the compassion, we can share, but in pain we are ultimately alone. The only real antidote is inside. The only real security is not insurance or money or a job, not a house and furniture paid for, or a retirement fund, and never is it another person. It is the skill and humor and courage within, the ability to build your own fires and find your own peace.

Audrey Sutherland, <u>Paddling My Own Canoe</u>

JANUARY 2009

TASMANIA IS AN ISLAND STATE off the southern coast of Australia. I remember watching cartoons of the "Tasmanian Devils" when I was growing up.

For more detail on maps, go to: http://still-going-strong.com

I was drawn to Tasmania for several reasons. I'd heard that Tasmania was similar to New Zealand with their tracks and hut system. Since I love backcountry travel in New Zealand, it seemed fitting that I explore Tasmania. Another reason was that I had just finished 14 months in Antarctica, and I really wanted to complete my experience of getting to all seven continents. Australia was the last one. So, in January of 2009, at age 63, I planned to explore Tasmania for three weeks.

An Unplanned Night Out

I booked a flight from Christchurch, New Zealand to Melbourne, Australia, before flying onto Hobart in Tasmania. When I arrived in Melbourne, I realized I had forgotten to bring my hiking poles. They were a key part of my gear since they held up my tent! Thankfully, I had a long layover and I was able to go shopping for new poles before catching my flight to Hobart.

My first stop was the Tasmanian District office to get maps and information on backcountry Tasmania. One of Tasmania's most famous tracks is the "Overland Track", also known as "Cradle Mountain. It is part of the Tasmanian World Heritage Wilderness and I was eager to see if I could hike it. Sometimes really popular hikes like Cradle Mountain, or the Milford Track in New Zealand, need to be booked a year in advance.

I asked at the District Office and was lucky enough to be able to book a trip starting in six days. I also had to book transport and lodging in order to shuttle from one end of the track to the other. Thankfully, the people in the office were very helpful and I was able to make all the arrangements right there and then. While I was at the office, I hired a Personal Locator Beacon. I usually used one whenever I was in New Zealand, and it made good sense to get one in Tasmania as well.

I had six days up my sleeve before starting the Overland Track, so I decided to explore other parts of this island. I started with a four-day trip at the Walls of Jerusalem Park. The park takes its name from the geological features within it that resemble the walls of the city of Jerusalem in Israel. As a result, many landmarks within the park also have Biblical references for names: Herod's Gate, Lake Salome, Solomon's Jewels, Damascus Gate, and the Pool of Bethesda.

There were designated camping areas at the park, as flat camping spots are few and far between. The first night at Wild Dog Creek, there were wooden platforms on which to "pitch" my tent and convenient "long drops". You get pretty used to these little houses when you go tramping! That first night I saw my first wild Wallabies. What a treat! They were very cute and I got photos of them right next to my tent.

Day Two took me to the other side of "the walls", where there was a hut. I believe it was one of the historical huts, and overnight use was prohibited except in case of emergency. I was happy to set up my tent anyway, as it was a pretty basic hut and I wouldn't have wanted to sleep in it. A woman has her standards, you know!

Day Three, and I day hiked to the closest peak and, of course, I climbed it! I really enjoyed the views from up there. Tasmania is not as big as New Zealand, but it is still beautiful in an Australian sort of way. I could see rows and rows of mountains in every direction I looked. On the final day, I hiked all the way back to my car.

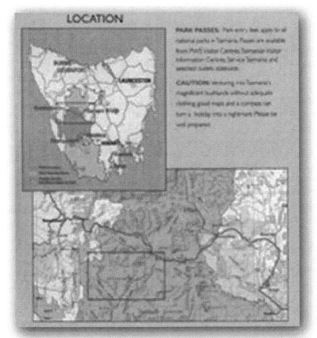

For more detail on maps, go to: http://still-going-strong.com

I still had a couple of days before I started the Overland Track, so I thought I would explore the area known as Frenchman's Cap. Because I didn't want to miss my Overland Track schedule, I decided I would just do a day hike up towards Frenchman's Cap. I based myself at a camping area near the Franklin River, and left my main backpack and most of my gear behind at camp. Armed with just a day-pack, I set off.

One of the portions on this trail is nicknamed the "Sodden Loddon", where the Loddon River makes the area a muddy bog. There were lots of side trails trying to go around the muddy spots so it had something of a braided appearance. I avoided some of the mud but I was still pretty filthy! Then the track climbed out of the boggy plains and up and over a ridge down to the Lake Vera Hut. The hut was in a lovely spot and equal to New Zealand standards.

I hiked up to the lake, which was a vivid blue color. I could see the mountains, the famous Frenchman's Cap, and the bush that came directly down to the lake. I had a quick lunch, but knowing I needed to get back to my gear and camping area, I turned around and headed back.

Since I didn't have a large pack, I was able to hike pretty fast. In the "Sodden Loddon" area, I bumped into a family with two kids. It was great to see young children out there, and I told them I was impressed. Right before we split up, I told them to not lose any small children in the mud, and I would try not to lose any old ladies in the mud. Very funny, Talie. Was that a premonition of things to come? Then I took off on one of the braided trails, to try to avoid the next mud hole.

Somewhere along these side trails, I got a little off the main track. I have since learned my lesson, and now when I am slightly off track, I just turn around and re-trace my steps to get back on the trail. But on this occasion, I thought I could go over the ridge, drop down into the riverbed, and head back down river to my camp spot.

Bad idea! I soon learned that bushwhacking in Tasmania is very detrimental to your body. I had some small gaiters on, as well as shorts, and I found out the bushes in Tasmania are really rough and scratchy, rather than feathery and friendly! I persevered and finally got to the river, following it down stream. I discovered that following a river in Tasmania is not the easiest thing to do either. I was slipping and sliding, going in and out of the water, around the worst of the bushes, and trying to find easier walking. The more I walked, the worse things got. At one point I realized I had lost my wristwatch. It must have been snagged off my arm by one of those man-eating bushes! And then, when I slipped in the water, I lost my reading glasses! Things were going from bad to worse. At least I still had my map, even if reading it was now a bit of a problem.

About this time, I realized the little emergency kit I ALWAYS carried with me, was in my backpack…and my backpack was back at my camp! In that kit was my compass, candle, pencil and paper, basic first aid kit, knife, knife sharpener, extra glasses, etc. My compass would have been really helpful along with those extra reading glasses. I kept struggling along, thinking my tent area would be just around the corner. It wasn't. Uh, oh – this was a serious bummer. Since I didn't have a flashlight, and because I wouldn't make it back to camp before dark, I realized I had better figure out a good place to spend the night.

I wanted to get away from the river and out of the thickness of the bushes. So I worked my way up a small hill and found a place under some larger trees, where the bushes weren't quite so thick. I thought I might find some ferns to make a bit of a shelter (am I remembering TV shows or what?). But since I didn't have a knife, I couldn't cut them. Then it was soon so dark, I could hardly see anything. I found a place that looked more comfortable than anywhere else, and settled down for the night.

When you don't have a candle, headlamp, or any other source of light, a night in the woods is DARK! Also, a night alone, in the woods is really LONG! So it was a very long, very dark night.

Another thing I learned about being in the woods of Tasmania overnight is this: the mosquitos are FIERCE! Luckily one of the few things I had with me was mosquito repellent. I also had an extra shirt, so I took off my damp shirt, and put it over my legs and put my dry shirt on my top along with my rain jacket. I hunkered into a small ball and tried to get a little sleep. I guess I dozed a couple of times. One time I woke up to a small animal scolding me:

"Ark! Ark! Ark!"

It might have been a Tasmanian Devil, but was probably just a possum. I apologized to him, but since I couldn't see him, I couldn't move out of his way! I was hoping he wouldn't get aggressive, and he finally wandered off.

After my long, dark night, it began getting light. I thought I must be close to my camp, so I tried following the river, but it became very twisted and turny! The brush was so thick in places that I had to put my hiking poles down in front of me and actually walk on the poles on top of the brush! After struggling and struggling, I finally thought, "Ok, enough of this!" With that, I broke away from the river and the thick bushes.

When I clambered out of the woods and got my bearings, I realized I had followed this river in a circle! Being on Crested Butte Search and Rescue for the last 10 years, I recognized a classic scenario, where lost people sometimes end up walking in a circle. I was not happy to now be doing that myself! But that negative mind set wouldn't do me any good. I had to keep my senses about me and figure out what to do next.

My legs were so scratched and bleeding, there was no way I could go through any more bushes. I headed out into the button grass area, and tried to get a bearing on where I might be. I designated a tree to be my "home base" (this is part of learning how "not to get lost"). I could see the weather was changing. Big dark clouds were starting to move pretty fast. I knew a storm was expected and those ominous clouds were signaling its onset.

I had been carrying EPRBs (Emergency Personal Rescue Beacons) all over New Zealand and Tasmania. I was tired, cold, shivering, and finally getting a little freaked out. Actually, looking back on it, I possibly had a mild case of hypothermia. So I pulled out the EPRB, and sat and looked at it...

"Well, ok. I guess this is the time!"

I turned it on.

"Beep,.. beep...beep...beep..."

The EPRB sent a signal up to a satellite that then relayed the signal to the Search and Rescue team in Tasmania.

I knew that once you activated a locator beacon, you were supposed to wait in one place until you were rescued. I waited for about an hour, but it was raining, and the longer I waited, the colder and wetter I became. I really needed to get moving to stop me from becoming more hypothermic. And the continuous beep-beep-beeping of the EPRB was driving me crazy!

I looked at the far ridge, and thought, "the trail must be between that ridge and where I am now." So my beacon and I beeped off in that direction. Fortunately, it was a matter of making my way in between the clumps of soft grasses, rather than scrub bushes. After half an hour of traveling, I spotted something white bobbing up and down ahead of me. It was a white hat. "OH MY GOSH that is a person on the trail! THERE IS THE TRAIL!" I headed for the white bobbing hat and came upon a couple of hikers. I was glad to see them and that beautiful muddy trail again!

Another thing I knew, was that once you have activated a rescue beacon, you were not supposed to turn it off. Well, I had been listening to this beep, beep, beep for about two hours, and to keep my sanity, I was going to HAVE to turn it off. Maybe, the troops weren't even on their way.

After another hour of hiking, I finally made it back to my original camp. I said good-bye to my new friends and they crossed the swing bridge to eat their lunch on the other side. I put my gear all back together, grabbed a bite to eat myself, and headed back toward my car.

After another half hour of hiking, I heard a helicopter. I assumed, correctly, that it was looking for me. Now what should I do? I decided my best plan was to hike to the trailhead, go to the nearest phone, and call someone to tell them I was ok. I kept heading up the trail toward the car park. I met some people on the trail who said, "It seems like that helicopter is looking for someone – your beacon didn't turn on by accident, did it?" I replied: "Yes, they are probably looking for me. I'm going to call them as soon as I can!"

As I got to the car park, the helicopter came in and landed. The pilot walked right up to me. "Is your name Natalie Morrison?" And my answer was, "Yes. I'm sorry!"

This nice Aussie pilot invited me to sit in the helicopter while we had a rather lengthy discussion. He had a medical officer with him who was more worried about my having a heart issue than my legs, which were TRASHED with scratches. I told them my story about getting lost and spending the night out, and my worries about the weather changing while I was still lost and possibly becoming hypothermic. They told me I should not have turned the beacon off (yes, I knew that) because they would continue to look for me thinking that maybe I had fallen into a river and that was why the beacon had stopped.

The helicopter crew were very professional and understanding of my plight. After our discussion, they fired up the helicopter and I waved as they flew off. It was really raining now, so I got in my car and headed to town.

Here's a footnote to this "misadventure". It's funny how fast things can go viral these days. Tasmanian Search and Rescue weren't the only people who knew I was missing. On the other side of the world, my son Craig was also right up with the play! I'll let him tell the story:

"I was driving down to LA for a meeting when my cell phone rang. The caller ID showed a very strange and long number, so I picked it up.

"Hello?"

A male with a very thick Australian accent replied, "Craig? This is Drew from Tasmanian Search and Rescue. Your Mum has gone missing and activated her search beacon."

I initially responded with stunned silence. So Drew continued, "We have sent a helicopter to find her and will ring you back when we have more information."

I then was able to at least compose myself enough to ask some questions, like how long has she been missing, and is there anything you need from me. I could hear myself trying to act like a "concerned son", but in the back of my mind I totally knew Mom was fine.

She was exactly where she wanted to be, and if anyone was going to be ok after going "missing" in the outback, it was her. Drew told me he would ring me back in a few hours, so I went on down to my meeting. After the meeting I checked my phone and saw that there were no calls. A few hours passed and no news. Now at this point, I am starting to get a little worried.

(But really not THAT much, I mean this is TALIE-MOM we are talking about...)

And when we finally got the news that all was well, and they had "found" my mum, I knew there was going to be a good story to hear the next time I spoke to Mom, and of course, she didn't disappoint..."

Onto The Overland

While I was out there in the bushes, one of my worries about being "rescued" was that I might miss my spot on the Overland Track. Oh, the things you think about in these situations. After all, I had paid the fees, the lodging, and the transportation costs, and I still wanted to do this famous track. Did I think a few dozen scratches would stop me? Of course not! I had to take extra care of some of the deepest scratches because I didn't want them to become infected while I was away from civilization. So, after getting food at the grocery store, I went to the pharmacy (drug store) and purchased betadine, antibiotic creams, band aids and anything else that might help. By the time I had finished the Overland Track, six days later, most of my scratches had healed up.

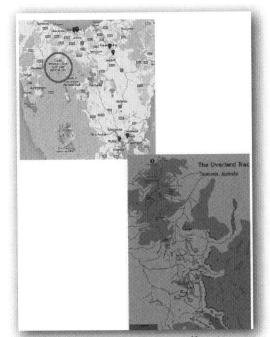

For more detail on maps, go to: http://still-going-strong.com

I arranged transport before the hike by leaving my little rental car at the terminus of the track (Lake St. Claire). I took a bus back to Hobart, another bus to Launceston, where I spent the night, and then an 8:00am bus to Cradle Mountain.

There were huts along the way, but it was recommended I carry a tent in case the huts were full. I had my Betamid tent with me, which is more like a rainfly than a tent. But it was relatively lightweight, and I could use my hiking poles to support it.

The first day promised to be hard work. This day had the biggest elevation gain, and my pack was at its heaviest, as it contained all my food for the week. I didn't get on the track until noon, and I wasn't sure I would be able to actually climb Cradle Mountain, as well as reach the hut. But it wasn't as bad as I thought; I was able to leave my pack on the trail and climb the mountain without it. There were some pretty fun bouldering sections, which reminded me of Colorado. And what a spectacular view from the summit! I even got to the first hut at the reasonable hour of 6:00pm and claimed a space on a bunk. That evening, the volunteer hut wardens saw me doctoring my legs and asked me, "What happened?" I explained my bushwhacking adventure, much to their amazement.

The next day, I passed by the Windermere Hut, as it was only a three hour walk. I didn't want to miss any of the short side hikes, and I didn't want to rush through the track. But on the other hand, I didn't want to sit around the huts either. Anyway, it was a long day, a 27 kilometer walk, plus a side trip to Lake Will. Despite the length of the walk, it was a wonderful day.

The Overland has beautiful Aussie bush. Lots of eucalyptus and manuka trees, which were all in bloom. There were plenty of improvements along the track, including a boardwalk, which not only made it easier to walk in some spots, but also protected the environment from boot steps. (They also ask you to use rubber tips if you have walking sticks.)

For five days, I hiked through the middle of Tasmania. I enjoyed the variety of forest and bush, and I loved bagging two peaks along the way: Cradle Mountain and Mount Ossa, the highest peak in Tasmania. From the top I saw miles and miles of bush! Now that I know how rough that bush is, I can appreciate it even more! During this hike, I was impressed how many of the walkers I encountered were Australians. Many had been planning this trip for years, and I felt honored to be amongst them.

At the end of the Tasmanian trip, I felt I had seen a good deal of the island. I'd had some awesome adventures, and had quite the "rescue" story to tell!

For more photos go to: http://still-going-strong.com

Alaska

● ● ●

You cannot stay on the summit forever
You have to come down again
So why bother in the first place?
Just this:
What is above knows what is below
but what is below does not know
what is above
One climbs, one sees. One descends, one sees
no longer, but one has seen.
There is an art of conducting oneself in the
lower regions by the memory of
what one saw higher up.
When one can no longer see, one can at least
still know.

Rene Daumal

EVER SINCE I HAD WINTERED in Alaska (back in the early 1990s), I had wanted to hike the Chilkoot Trail. The trail straddles the USA and Canada, and getting permits was a bit daunting. This trip actually became a real concept while I was in Antarctica. My adventurous friends in Crested Butte decided they would like to hike the Chilkoot. They emailed me and asked if I would like to join them. I was excited to hike with them, so I went on the internet and booked airline tickets for July 2008.

At that time, I thought I would only be in Antarctica for six months, from August till February. However, I decided to stay for the polar winter which lasted until October. So, I called Alaska Airlines and they said I had credit for that ticket for 12 months after the original travel date. That meant I could use it until July of 2009. Great!

July 2009

At Last! Following the Chilkoot Trail

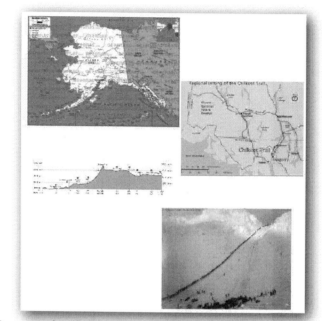

For more detail on maps, go to: http://still-going-strong.com

After 14 months in Antarctica, I got home to the USA in May of 2009. July is the most beautiful month of the summer in Crested Butte and it was hard for me to leave. But I had credit on this airline ticket and I didn't want to lose that, so I booked to go to Alaska.

While I had been in Santa Barbara, I'd had breakfast with one of my dear friends, Jaye. I told her about my trip to Alaska, and she asked if she could come along. She didn't want to hike the trail, but she did want to hang out in Skagway and see the area. Jaye made reservations to get to Alaska from Santa Barbara and we met up in Seattle. From Seattle, we flew into Juneau, and then by small plane into Skagway. Jay had booked a cabin since she would be spending six nights in Skagway and I shared the cost for the first and last nights. The next morning, Jaye drove me to the trailhead for the Chilkoot Trail.

When I plan a trip like this, there are so many things to think about, plus the apprehension of going alone into the wilderness…and in this case, into serious bear country. I do a lot of worrying, which no one seems to notice but me. But by the time I am actually on the trail, my whole body lets out a huge sigh of relief. I am, once again, back in the arms of Nature.

Before I left Crested Butte, I had to decide what kind of shelter I would use at night. Pack weight is a big issue for me. Too much slows me down, but too little might mean I don't have enough survival gear. I didn't want to carry the weight of a full tent, and my little blue tarp was still in New Zealand. So, I got some scraps of silicone treated nylon and pieced them together to make a large, but lightweight, tarp-like shelter. I could fit both my sleeping bag and my backpack under it; a good thing because I knew Alaska could be wet as well as cold. I wasn't worried about not having a bottom to my shelter, since there wouldn't be many "creepy crawlies" up there. And my sleeping bag "system" was waterproof on the bottom. (This system is a homemade sleeping bag that has insulation only on the top and sides. The bottom of the bag is just an envelope of two pieces of silicone treated nylon. My sleeping pad fits into the envelope thus protecting me from the cold ground. The pad actually becomes part of the sleeping bag.)

Because the Chilkoot Trail is so popular, you need a permit to hike it. There are designated campsites you have to stay in. This mitigates the impact on the environment, and also allows for some sort of food storage to prevent bear encounters. I had to decide which campsites I would use before I set off. In an emergency I could switch campsites, but normally I had to stay where I had agreed to camp. This would allow the authorities to regulate how many people were in the camping areas every night.

Jaye walked with me for a couple of hours at the beginning of the trail. After lunch, she headed back to the car, while I continued on. The portion of trail Jaye and I did together was pretty mellow, but after that lunch stop, it started getting rough, with lots of ups and downs. Even so, I reached the first campsite about 4:00pm and set up my shelter for the night. There was a little cabin (not for sleeping) where I could cook my dinner on a table, out of the weather. The cabin had interesting artifacts, relics, and information about the miners during the gold rush.

While I was cooking my dinner, I met some of the other hikers doing the trail. When people saw my Pepsi-can stove, which was another homemade item, they almost always commented on it. Thus my little stove was a conversation starter, and invariably, people got round to asking lots of questions about my solo hiking, and my unusual gear. It was a great way to get to know people, and I was relieved that my chosen gear for this trip would probably be functional.

The next day, I headed up the valley following a beautiful trail into some rugged country, with lots of trees and bushes…and lots of places for bears to be sitting. The one thing you don't want to do in bear country is surprise a bear. If a bear hears you coming it will most likely run away, unless it is eating a dead animal or has cubs. So the standard practice in bear country is to make lots of noise when you are walking through the woods and bushes. That's a bit easier when you're with other people, but can be challenging when you're hiking alone.

I carried on a conversation with the bears. "Hey bear, Hey bear - Here I come" and sometimes I would sing. Sure, I wouldn't have made it very far on American Idol, but maybe the bears don't care! On the whole Chilkoot Trail, I didn't see any bears, so either they weren't there, or my singing scared them away. Being in bear country does make you constantly apprehensive about what might be out there. You are hiking in places where you are NOT the top of the food chain.

The next night's campsite was the last one before the pass. Because it was still relatively low in altitude, and it was July, the temperatures were quite mild and not below freezing yet. I set up my new home and went for a short hike up the trail where I would continue tomorrow. It was pretty cloudy and I couldn't see all the way up to the pass, but I could get some feel for what it might be like the next day. On this excursion, I met three girls from Canada who were also doing the Chilkoot. We totally connected and I am still in touch with them. When you meet people out on these remote and rugged trails, they are just the most awesome people. I think it is because they love doing the same things I love doing.

The morning of climbing the Golden Stairs (the trail leading up to Chilkoot Pass) started out misty and rainy, and deteriorated from there. After an hour or so on the trail, I pulled out my new Go Lite umbrella. This piece of gear was suggested to me by a group that did the Chilkoot the year before. It is a lightweight, but strong, plastic umbrella so it doesn't add a lot of weight to your pack. It was wonderful. It kept my head and shoulders dry, so I could have my jacket open and ventilate a bit more. I got even more comments from fellow hikers about that particular piece of gear!

Along the trail, there were discarded items from the old miners, and placards describing what life was like back then. There were interpretive signs and information on how the area was used as a "staging" for miners carrying their gear to the top of the pass. The Canadian government did not want all these miners on their way to the gold fields to be in Canada and dying from exposure and starvation during the harsh winters. So the Royal Mounties would not let the miners into Canada unless they had 1000 pounds of gear with them.

Thus the miners would make many trips to the base of the Golden Stairs, piling up their gear. Then they would make multiple trips up the pass (some of them carried almost 200 pounds a trip), and when it was all piled up at the top, they would basically sled it down the other side. I already knew this, but it was still interesting to see the terrain they had gone over. It was also fascinating to see old photos and pieces of equipment – wheels, boxes, and even discarded shoes. It was a good thing there were pictures of the pass because it was raining so hard, I sure couldn't see it!

Since it was the middle of summer, the Golden Stairs was not full of snow like the photos depicted. That was OK with me. It was actually a large boulder field, going almost straight up to the pass. By climbing peaks in Colorado, I had learned all about boulder fields, thus this one didn't scare me very much.

As I headed up the Golden Stairs, I found that I couldn't use my umbrella. It was so steep, the umbrella prevented me from seeing what was above me, so I tucked it back into my pack. There were a couple of guys behind me that I could occasionally see coming through the fog, but mostly I was alone going up this giant boulder field. I guess if you weren't used to boulder fields, this would have seemed daunting. There was even a path of sorts in and around some of the boulders. But the weather was not co-operating: it was very rainy and damp cold. With my pack weighing about 35 pounds, I could feel real sympathy for those miners who were slogging up this pass with 200 pounds on their backs. Up, up, up I went. This reminded me of trails in New Zealand - straight up!

In one of the descriptions I had read about the Chilkoot Trail, it said to listen for the snap of the flag at the border as you'd likely not see it. I guess being in fog is more common than not! The flag would be at the Mountie's station, which marked the border between Canada and the USA. Sure enough, I could hear it snapping before I could see it. Right next to it was a beautiful little cabin, and even better than that, I saw a Mountie with a thermos of hot chocolate in his hand. He invited me to come in and warm up. Since I was shivering, that was a lovely thing! It felt so good to be out of the cold and rain.

I was the first person to stop at the Mountie's station, but other climbers started coming in and the room was soon filled with wet, cold trampers. With all that moisture, it got really steamy inside. I felt I should give up my space for others, so I put on my rain gear and headed back out into the elements.

The Mountie Station marked the border between the USA and Canada, but it was not quite at the top of the pass. I still had some climbing to do. The weather continued to be pretty uncooperative - windy, cloudy, and rainy - but the route was marked with snow poles. There were lots of snowfields to cross this high in the mountains, and it was a bit spooky not being able to see where a field ended. If I slipped, I didn't know if I would I end up on some rocks, or splash down into a lake, or slide for thousands of feet. It was a scary feeling, so I made sure I had solid footsteps under me in the snow.

I was really wishing it would clear up so I could actually see more of this beautiful area, but that was not to happen that day. What I could see, though, was awesome. Patches of snow, clear-water running creeks, tarns and lakes, and alpine tundra plants and grasses. All it needed was a little sunshine. But then, sunny days up here were few and far between!

Up and down, round and back, snow and rock, trail and grasses. It was all of those things until I got to the next campsite. I was tired. It had been a long, cold day. This campsite had a hut for cooking and warming up, but still no sleeping inside. So I set up my tarp and got my stove, dinner and tea and headed to the hut. I was definitely not the only one in there. It was packed! I found a little spot to fix my dinner, then gave my place up for someone else. A short while later, I went back in and fixed another cup of tea to help stay warm. By this time it was pretty steamy in there, but the warmth felt good.

Even with the damp and cold at the higher altitude, my makeshift tent worked just fine. I could peg it down closer to the ground for more warmth when the wind was blowing, or have it a bit off the ground when I needed the wind to prevent condensation. And I was loving the fact that it was so lightweight!

That night it cleared off. How I wished it had been like this going up the pass! The trail started out in this beautiful alpine tundra, following the rivers that the miners had used to boat their gear down to the lakes. There were some pretty intense rapids, and stories abound about miners getting this far, only to have their boats, and all their gear, smashed to bits in the rapids. By hiking this far, in the footsteps of those miners who carried 1000 pounds of gear, only to have their hopes and dreams dashed, I was inspired to think about what a tough bunch of people they were. And what hopes they had of becoming rich! It is amazing what we humans will do for the sake of gold!

Because it was over the tops and along the rivers, the hiking on day four was relatively easy. Thus I got to the next campsite fairly early in the day. I had thought this might happen when I got my permit, and arranged with the rangers that if I got to a campsite early enough, I could go on to the next one. It made for a long day, but it would make the next day that much shorter. Besides, on my last day I had a deadline to meet. I needed to get to the station to catch the train back to Skagway! Jaye would come up on the train to meet me.

I arrived at the next campsite late in the day. It overlooked a lovely lake so I was doubly glad that I had gone on. There was an open shelter, with tables for cooking, but luckily it wasn't raining. All of the other campsites had "lock boxes" for overnight food storage to minimize bear encounters, but this campsite had a pole high in the air on which to hang your food. I had brought a rope for just this possibility.

The final morning was a much different type of hiking. It was so dry that the trails were actually dusty. I was interviewed by a camera crew making a promotional film for Canada. They said they would email me if I made it into the film. I never heard back from them. Bummer!

As I came over the hill to see Lake Bennett, (the end of the trail), I also could see the train pulling into the station. Perfect timing. I went down to the station and located Jaye having lunch with the other train riders. The hikers had a place to have lunch too, but it was separated from the train passengers. I guess they figured we might be too dirty and rambunctious for the more sedate train riders! Thankfully, they did let me in to see Jaye, and most of her new friends from the train were impressed!

We had a couple of hours before the train departed, so we explored the Lake Bennett area, seeing more remnants of the gold rush along with the old church, which was still standing. Then we got on the train bound for Skagway. Yikes! That rail bed was cut directly out of the rocks, and clung to the side of the mountains. My acrophobia was kicking in big time. Not such a fright for Jaye. She'd seen it on the way up, and knew what to expect. What a ride!

After a day in Skagway, we flew back to Juneau. It was a rainy, windy day and I was freaked out about flying in a little bitty plane. I wanted to back out, but I couldn't. I knew these little planes could take a lot, and the pilots wouldn't fly if it weren't safe, but I was still scared. I was not happy with myself as I had worked myself into a real tizzy. I got on the plane and tried to calm myself, succeeding somewhat. By the time we were coming into Juneau, I was finally OK. Here I was, this fearless backpacker, acting like a little scaredy cat about flying home. I found the irony of it pretty funny…eventually!

For more photos go to: http://still-going-strong.com

South America

● ● ●

A happy person is not a person in a certain set of circumstances,
but rather a person with a certain set of attitudes.

Robert Holden, Ph.D.

IN 2007, I STARTED DEVISING a travel plan for South America. I had
several things I especially wanted to see: Machu Picchu, Patagonia,
Ushuaia, and Tierra del Fuego. I even took Spanish lessons. Then, all
of a sudden, I was going to Antarctica! My South America trip was put
on hold.

After 14 months in Antarctica, and then eight months in New Zealand,
I finally got back to Crested Butte. Then, I had to use my air ticket to
Alaska for the Chilkoot trail. Once I got back from there, I could finally
put my South America trip back on track.

I booked a flight to Lima, Peru, and a return ticket from Buenos Aires,
Argentina. I had four months between these flights to travel through Peru,
Chile, and Argentina.

November 2009

Adventures in Peru

My first country in South America was Peru. I visited Machu Picchu, Lake Titicaca, and Arequipe, all of which were very impressive and beautiful!

I was travelling on a bus to the southern Peruvian town of Tacna. On the bus I met a really friendly Australian lady, Robin. She was my age, and also going to Tacna. We ended up booking into the same hostel. We even decided to go out to dinner together. Because it was early in the night, we were the only ones in the restaurant, and were seated in the middle of the room. A man came in and said we had to move because of the television. He kept pointing to another table and shaking the chairs. Then, abruptly, he left.

After watching this crazy fellow, I turned back to the table and noticed my daypack, which had been right next to me, was gone! Robin and I both yelled "THIEF!!", and ran outside the restaurant. There was a policeman on the street, but the thief and his accomplice, who I had not even laid eyes on 'til that point, disappeared into the crowd and fled in a taxi.

Aargh! I totally got suckered into that one! You often hear about thieves creating a distraction in order to steal something; that's exactly what had happened to me. While the crazy guy was shaking chairs and diverting our attention away from our table, his unseen co-thief was taking my pack. Luckily, I had my credit cards and cash in my pocket, but the daypack contained my camera, which was full of photos, and my passport. What a bother!!!!

So, take it from one who knows. Here's what you have to do if your passport is stolen in a foreign country. First, locate your country's embassy and plan on going there. In my case, I had to book a flight to Lima, spend a night in a hotel there, and then take a taxi to the American Embassy. While I waited, the Embassy issued a temporary passport that was good for 30 days.

Now, when most people have their passport stolen while overseas, they're ready to call it quits and head home. Not me. I was on the first month of a four-month South American adventure, and I wasn't going to let those thieving jerks spoil my fun! So I got my 30 day passport, and used it to get from Peru to Santiago, Chile. There I went to the American Embassy and applied for a permanent passport. The process would take 30 days, as the paperwork had to go to the USA and back to Chile. That wasn't a problem, as long as I didn't leave Chile. It was a stunning country, with lots of places to explore, so it wasn't a hardship to stay for that long.

Once I got my permanent passport, I was good to go. I finished exploring Chile. I booked 3 days on the Navimag which took me down the coast of Chile and then hiked the track around the Torres del Paine. Then I headed to Ushuaia, Argentina.

JANUARY 2010

A TASTE OF TIERRA DEL FUEGO
Ushuaia is the capital city of the province of Tierra del Fuego, located in front of the Beagle Channel and surrounded by the Martial Mountains, along the bay that gave it its name. It has been translated as "the bay that penetrates west".

For more detail on maps, go to: http://still-going-strong.com

The combination of mountains, forest and sea makes it a unique city in Argentina. An irregular topography gives it a picturesque appearance, made even more distinctive by the colorful houses built mainly from wood and corrugated iron. It is surrounded by a series of Natural Protected Areas and is one of the most active gateways to Antarctica.

It is the southernmost urban area in the world, a source of inspiration and challenges, a land of myths and legends, even for those who have never been to the south of the south. I immediately fell in love with Ushuaia. I loved the flowers in its gardens and parks, and I found the people to be very friendly. Sure, it is a tourist town, but it is still wonderful!

Tierra del Fuego was formerly the name given to the lands south of the Straits of Magellan. Today, the name is applied to the archipelago formed by a main island, and hundreds of lesser isles south to Cape Horn and east to Staten Island. The name is used in Argentina and Chile, since the islands are a shared territory. Outside of Ushuaia is the Tierra del Fuego National Park, which I thought would be a good representation of the area. Unfortunately, the cost and inaccessibility of the National Park was a real let down for me. It cost 50 pesos to take a bus to the park, and another 50 pesos to get in. There were a few trails around the inlets, but I felt very deflated. I had come so far to experience this area, but I was pretty limited in what I could see.

In my wanderings around Ushuaia, I had noticed an "Officia de Guias" (Office of Guides). I was hoping to get out of town for a couple of days and into the National Park. The guide office was very helpful. They sold me a map and showed me a wonderful hike that went over the "Paso de la Oveja" (Pass of the Sheep). The guide told me there was a designated camping area at a high mountain lake. This looked like a perfect hike to get out into the National Forest of Terre del Fuego! I could have done it in one night, but decided to spend two nights out.

For more detail on maps, go to: http://still-going-strong.com

I asked the hostel I was staying in to call me a taxi. I also told them I would be back in a couple of nights, and booked a bed for when I returned.

That way I could leave my extra gear at the hostel. The taxi picked me up and we headed out of town. The taxi driver didn't speak English, but I showed him where I was going on the map and he understood perfectly. He kept giving me funny looks in the rear view mirror, and finally he said, "Solo?" Well, that was understandable in any language! And I said, "Si." He thought about that a minute and figured I hadn't understood, so he asked again, "Solo?" I laughed and told him "Si!" Shaking his head he then asked me. "Cuántos años tiene Usted?" He was asking how old I was! I told him I was 63. He was really shaking his head now!

After I got out of the taxi, I headed up the trail. Well, I was hoping it was the trail since there were no signs! The taxi driver didn't leave till I was almost out of sight. I guess he figured I would come running back and want to go back to town!

It was a grey and cloudy day, but I was well equipped and happy to be backpacking in the mountains. This first part of the trail was actually an old dirt road. I came upon a herd of horses and they shared the trail with me. I wasn't sure if they were wild horses or part of a ranch.

As I worked my way up into the mountains, it became more of a trail, which, for me, is preferable to walking on a road. I was going along quite happily when all of a sudden, in the middle of the trail, I came across a sign:

"Sendero Cerrado! Trail Closed! No Trespassing!"

I couldn't even pretend I didn't understand what the sign meant since it was also in English. I figured the trail must go off another way, so I headed up to the left and got into some really rough bush bashing. So, I tried the other side. There was no trail there either, just more forest! Now what?

I'd been hiking for an hour and going back wasn't an option. Besides, my friendly taxi driver was probably back in Ushuaia telling people about this crazy American lady who took off by herself and would probably never be seen again! So, I decided to push on up the trail and see why it was closed. It seemed to me that if the whole trail was closed, the company of guides would have told me. Or there would have been a sign at the trailhead – or what I thought was the trailhead!

I was pretty confused. There is a saying that I chose to follow here: "Better to beg forgiveness than to ask for permission." So on I went. The trail seemed fine. I could see no reason why it should be closed. My map showed the trail going between a river on my right, and a mountain on my left. As long as I didn't cross the river or climb the mountain, I couldn't get lost! So I continued on….

I met a couple of Brits coming the other way down the trail. They asked if I had seen the sign. I told them I had. They told me a story they had heard of a couple that walked past the sign and almost to the lake, only for a ranger to find them. He was very angry they had passed his sign and made them walk all the way back. The two Brits had decided to hike this trek in the opposite direction since there wasn't a sign closing it on the other side. Now, that was thinking "outside the box"!

I was a little nervous about bumping into Señor Ranger. But I figured if I could just get up to the lake, and the designated camping area, then if a ranger came by, I could tell him I had come in the other way. I asked the Brits how far it was to the lake and they estimated about three hours (whew, were they ever off – even as slow as I am going up a hill, it took only half that time for me). The going got quite steep coming out of the forest, but then I was above the tree-line and much happier. There is definitely something about being on an alpine trail that makes my spirits soar.

The trail was steep and the wind had picked up, but it was easy to follow and I could see where it was leading. As I topped out over the ridge,

I got a glimpse of the lake where I would be camping. It was beautiful up there!!! After another 15 minutes of climbing, the trail headed down to the lake. Going up had been steep, as was going down to the lake, so I sometimes slid down on my rear end. Before I could get to the camping area, I had to cross a small stream. There wasn't a bridge, so in the interest of having semi-dry boots, I took off my boots and socks and waded across the stream. Burrr!!!

Now I could let go of the stress of meeting the ranger, and really enjoy where I was. I set up my tarp/tent, pegging it down on the side where the wind was coming from. I had a lovely dinner of pasta, tuna, and tea, and continued to enjoy this tranquil spot. It would have been even more tranquil if the wind hadn't been blowing so hard, but you can't have everything! Wandering around the edge of the lake with my after dinner cup of tea, I watched a beaver swimming around. He smacked his tail several times and dove down into the water, which entertained me immensely!

The next day, I explored the countryside above my little lake. The day continued to be windy, but I had plenty of layers and was relatively comfortable. I learned in Alaska that when the blowing wind started to drive me crazy, I should just think of it as the earth breathing. There were lots of interesting plants that grew at that high altitude, and I was fascinated by them as they were so different from Colorado. Lots of them I had never seen before and, of course, I had no idea what their names were. Sometimes I think I can enjoy the natural world more if I <u>don't</u> know the names of plants. Anyway, I had a lovely day of solitude and communing with nature.

Day three was a delight. Not a puff of wind and clear, blue skies. As I didn't have an extra day's food, I had to leave this amazing place. Reluctantly, I packed my gear, and headed back up the slippery-slidy trail. The route headed up to the actual Paso de la Oveja. I had more snow to cross but it wasn't very steep and most of the trail was clear. Remember that wind that wasn't at my camp site that morning? I guess it had decided to hang out up at the pass! Whew, it was blowing hard!

Once I was off the pass, the wind died down and I enjoyed the scenery. The trail was well marked, but it was on a very exposed slope. The whole hillside was scree and the trail was just a bit of a level spot going across it. It reminded me of a trail outside of Crested Butte going to Yule Pass. Even the other side of the valley looked just like Yule Pass. Interesting that I was so far away, with different flora and fauna, but traversing similar landscapes.

It was a lovely route back down around the mountains and directly into the town of Ushuaia. I walked right through town and back to the hostel from which I had started. I felt like I had experienced just a little bit of the real Tierra del Fuego, and was glad I never met up with the ranger who put up the closed sign.

FEBRUARY 2010

REFUGIO TO REFUGIO TO REFUGIO...
From Ushuaia I headed up Argentina. . My Canadian friend Therese, who I had met and hiked with in Antarctica, joined me in Argentina. We hiked up to see Mt. Fitzroy and then we ended up in Baraloche for several multi-day hikes including the Curicuito Chico. Baraloche has a lovely ski area and some great hiking. Then Therese headed back to Buenos Aires and I headed to El Bolson.

El Bolson is a small mountain town in the Patagonia region of Argentina The people in Baraloche refer to El Bolson as a "hippy town". That made me want to see it even more! So, as Therese headed back to Canada, I headed to El Bolson.

For more detail on maps, go to: http://still-going-strong.com

As usual, I was flying by the seat of my pants, and I didn't book ahead in El Bolson. So when the bus stopped, I went to the tourist center and got a list of local hostels. I walked around town until I found a delightful hostel that had space for me. I ended up staying there, off and on, for about two weeks and it became a great base. I had picked up a head cold and spent the first few days laying low and recuperating.

I wanted to do a three-day trip into the mountains, going to Refugio Hielo Azul and Refugio Canon Azul. I had, for once, been a responsible backcountry hiker and had signed out with the CAP (local clearing house for backpacker trips). The trip up to Hielo Azul was a climb of 1000 meters (about 3000 feet). When the hostel owner heard I was heading into the mountains in the rain, complete with my sniffles and cough, he read me the riot act …in Spanish! From what I understood, he was seriously concerned about my health, and probably my sanity. Of course, whenever an older man tells me what to do, my first reaction is "Just watch me!" I had been staying in town and watching it rain for four days. I was over it. I needed to get out!

Off to the bus I went. I pointed to my map and asked the driver if he stopped where the CAP map said I should start. He said he would let me know when we were there. Of course, as was typical of my South American adventures, he dropped me off in the middle of a dirt road with no signs or anything. I watched the bus go on about 200 meters and drop off another passenger who went down a side road. Well, that looked good to me too, as I knew the river was down that way, and my trail went alongside the river. What could go wrong?

Getting to the trail was hit and miss, but eventually I found one that seemed to go where my map indicated it should. I had been told not to cross the first bridge across Rio Azul but to go to the second bridge instead. I'm glad I remembered that or I could have been off on an adventure I was not wanting!

Yes, the trail was up, up, up! Almost 3000 feet up! It was sprinkling off and on most of the day, but I had my "Go Lite" umbrella and used it when I needed to. I really felt that getting out in the fresh and humid air was doing my cold good. I never saw anyone else on the trail. Since I love being in the mountains alone, that was just fine with me.

When I got to Refugio Hielo Azul, a young American exchange student, Catherine, was already there. Later, five young people from Buenos Aires showed up. They were celebrating a birthday and were in the mood to party. I let them use my little tripod so they could get group photos after I went to bed. Being a solo hiker, a tripod is a good piece of gear to have, since when I am on the top of a mountain, there is usually no one else to take my photo. The tripod has saved my camera from falling over, or falling off a mountain, while I run around in front of it!

The next morning. Catherine and I climbed the rest of the mountain to see Glacier Azul and the small lake in front of it. The refugio keepers had given us a map to follow. Catherine hiked back down since she had to work her way back to Valparaiso in Chile to start her semester abroad. I decided it would be good to bake in the sun to finish healing my cold. It was a delightful spot, and I planned on spending two nights at the refugio.

Mid-afternoon, I hiked back down to the refugio, only to find out a group of 40 more people were expected for the night. The birthday group had decided to go on to another refugio, about three hours away, but I thought I would stay. When the new group showed up, it was the Baraloche Hiking Club. Most of the hikers were in their 40s and 50s – whew, much better than 40 teenagers! There were about 10 others staying there who weren't in the Baraloche group, so it was a full refugio that night. The refugio keepers were a young couple with two small children, and it was amazing to watch them fix dinner and breakfast for 40 hungry hikers! I knew it was big money for them, and it is how they survive, but they were still amazing! I had my own food, so at least I was not an extra mouth for them to feed.

The next morning, I hiked on to Refugio Natation, saying 'Hi" to the birthday group who had stopped there. I had a cup of tea and left my backpack while I hiked above that refugio to check out the area. There were glorious snowfields, with a stream running under them. I thought I would hike above the snowfields to see if there was a lake further up. The next thing I knew, I was pulling myself hand over hand from small trees on the side of a really steep slope. How did I get myself into this mess?! On top of all that, there wasn't a lake up there anyway! So I slip-slided down, hand over hand, and berated myself for doing something I shouldn't have. But I didn't hurt myself, so thank you again, Guardian Angels!

After collecting my gear from Refugio Natation, off I went towards Canon Azul. It was a beautiful ridge through the forest, with lakes here and there. Then I came around the corner to see where the trail would go down to the river. It looked steep. I stopped to have lunch and take a break, as there was no sense getting to the refugio too early. It was a lovely rocky perch with a glorious view down the valley.

On the trail through the woods I had been "leap frogging" with a couple from Australia. The Aussies passed me while I was having lunch. It sounded like she was having a bit of a problem with the steepness. I offered her one of my hiking poles but she said the stick she was using was enough help. Then another solo female hiker passed me by. Her name was Annie and she was from Germany. She also was dealing with the steepness as her knees were hurting, but at least she had hiking poles.

After a nice break, I also took off down the slope. It was a bit steep, but I was usually OK with downhills. Soon I passed by the Aussies, and then I came upon Annie who was resting alongside the track. She asked if I was going to go on to the second refugio: Retamal. It was supposed to be more beautiful and was only 45 minutes further on. Hmmm... that sounded good. So when I got to Refugio Canon Azul, I stopped for a cup of tea (refugios almost always had a pot of hot water on the stove), and then hiked on up the trail. That 45 minutes was more like 90 minutes, but it was still early enough when I arrived. I occasionally saw Annie in front of me - she must have passed me while I was having my tea.

As I was hiking, I saw a nice soft-shell jacket lying on the trail. It brought up a question in my mind: When you see something by the side of the trail, should you take it, or leave it there? Personally, I think you should take it on. Rarely does someone know they have lost something, and usually people are not willing to retrace their steps to retrieve it. If they are coming back, you usually see them on the trail anyway. So I picked it up, and took it to the next refugio. When I got there, I held up the jacket and asked if anyone was missing it. Sure enough, a girl claimed it – she was glad I had brought it to her.

Retamal was a GREAT refugio. They had home brewed beer! I was certainly glad I hiked the extra way to get there. Plus, I got to know Annie a bit better. She was from Munich, Germany. She spoke English like a native, and was a delightful girl. When I say girl, I don't actually know her age, but I would guess somewhere in the 20s!

Annie was talking about another refugio much further up the trail, Los Laguitos. (The Little Lakes). She asked if I wanted to go there. I told her I had signed out with CAP and they planned on me being back the next day. We found out the refugio keepers were in contact with CAP by radio and they could tell them I had continued on. My other problem was that I only brought enough food for four days, but that was solved when I realized I could purchase food at the refugios. For once, I was a responsible hiker and set down a plan – and then I totally changed the plan. That's the reason I usually don't set down the plan in the first place!

Bright and early the next morning, Annie and I headed up the trail to Los Laguitos. Most of the day was alongside a river, with a couple of detours away from it. Following a river is always interesting, because you think it will be level. But when cliffs come down to the edge of the river, you have to leave the riverbed and go up and over, then down the other side to the river bank.

We stopped for lunch on a rocky sandbar by the river, and along came two "caballeros" (cowboys). They crossed the river on their horses without stopping to talk, but it was sure interesting to see them. It made me feel like I was really in South America!

During another break, Annie asked if I wanted a matte. Matte is drunk all over South America, and there's a ritual that goes with it. It is a tea, of sorts, actually called: Yerba Matte. It does have some caffeine in it, but they say it is a better type of stimulant than coffee or tea. The "instruments" of matte are: a cup – which usually is a gourd but can be made of leather or wood, a straw or bombilla which is metal and usually has a strainer at the end, a thermos of hot water and, of course yerba matte in loose form. First in goes the bombilla, and then you pour some matte in the cup, then a little water. You work the bombilla down to the bottom, making a small "hole" in the matte, and then add more hot water.

The ritual is that the person who has made the matte drinks the first cup. Then they pour in more hot water to make another cup and passes it to the next person. When they have finished, they pass it back to the maker and more hot water is added and it is passed to the next person, and so on. Everyone eventually gets their cup of matte as it is passed around the group. Thus, I learned to drink matte by the side of a river surrounded by trees, plants and mountain peaks!

Along the way to Los Laguitos, we were supposed to come upon some Alerce trees. These incredible trees are related to California Redwoods, and some are thought to be 4000 years old! Our map showed a section of the trail that just said "Alerces" and we hoped we would recognize the trees. Well, of course, we recognized them. We needed to stop and hug them, and take our photos hugging them. I even lay on the ground and took some photos looking up the tree. I was surprised at the softness of their bark – it was almost spongy and was falling off in some spots.

I loved being among these old trees with my new friend, Annie. Even though there is probably 40 years difference in our ages, we are kindred spirits on this planet. It is amazing how you meet some people and form an instant bond. As much as I love hiking solo, this was a special treat to have such a loving companion to walk with me.

Along the trail, we met a man coming down. He had a bandage over a bad cut on his hand, and was going back to the doctor to have it checked. That meant he had a 10-hour hike to receive medical attention (at least at the speed I hike – for him it was probably only a five hour hike!). We had a great chat. Annie had a much better handle on Spanish than me, and he said to say "hello" to the folks looking after the next refugio. We later found out he was the refugio keeper and it was his wife and child who were still there taking care of the place!

The refugio was a welcome sight. Sure enough, the wife and baby daughter were taking care of it. Amber, the four-month old baby, was having a rough time of it. I got a chance to hold her in order to give her mom a break. That was an added treat for me – using a little "grandma energy"! Amber seemed to like me holding her, so I took over whenever I could, especially when her mom fixed us a yummy pizza! As you will remember, I was supposed to be back in town by now, so the food I had brought was pretty much depleted. Annie and I also bought some bread for breakfast and lunch.

The next morning, a clear day greeted us. You would not believe the beauty! The lake in front of the refugio was totally calm and had a perfect reflection of the mountains on the other side. It was a picture postcard scene. Annie and I wandered around taking photos and whispering. It was too spiritual to speak out loud! I am always so thankful when I am in places like this, at times like this. It makes any hardships along the trail totally worth it! I guess that is what keeps me going on these crazy trips of mine!

After much tea drinking, breakfast eating, and baby holding, Annie and I headed back down the track. Our plan was to retrace our steps down the trail and go on to the Refugio Encanto Blanco. This trail was not marked on the map but we had been told about it at the last refugio. The word was: "it is very steep for about 45 minutes". "Ok", I thought, "I could handle that." So after giving our friends the Alerce trees more hugs, we came to a sign pointing towards Valle de Encanto. Sure enough it was steep, very steep, and rough as well. After 90 minutes we were still going up! Well, I must admit, we did do a little sidetrack, which was even scarier. I told Annie we should retrace our steps and find the real trail, which was marked with little red ribbons. Being back on the real trail, even though it was rough, was much better than bashing our way through the bush. Maybe I did learn something from being lost in Tasmania!

While we were still going up, I finally had to stop and eat something. We had thought we would reach the top before lunch, but my body was about to hit the wall. I needed to get some fuel on board. That was a good move and made the rest of the climb much better. We finally reached the top and the trail took us through the woods before going down the other side into the next valley. This valley seemed to be full of South American bamboo, so we felt like we were walking through a maze of bamboo with little tunnels cut through them. Finally we reached the Rio Blanco, and then the refugio, which was in yet another beautiful spot.

Please indulge me as I write a little side note again. Remember how I found that soft-shell jacket on the trail? The girl who claimed it in Retamal had a very young child...only about two years old. I was amazed to see her, and her baby, way up there at the Refugio Encanto Blanco. She had a "baby backpack", so she carried the baby in the pack and her gear was carried beneath the baby. Thankfully, a friend was able to carry some of her gear, but I still could not believe that they had come over the same horrendous trail the day we went up to Los Legatos. Got to love these outdoor people!

The refugio keeper in Encanto Blanco made me a delicious cheese veggie casserole for dinner, and we bought more homemade bread and, of course, had some matte. The next morning we hiked back up the valley a little to see a waterfall. We found a lookout with views up the whole valley, so it was the perfect place to hang out before we started our hike to the road.

Hiking out, we missed a turn somewhere and found ourselves on an old trail with no markers. The further we went, the more nervous we got, but at least we were heading to the river. Then, after about an hour on this mystery trail, we met a couple of men on horseback. They confirmed we were on the wrong trail, and said we were heading towards a dead end. (It was a good thing Annie understood Spanish). The guys kindly led us through the woods until we were at the real trail.

Once we crossed the river, we had about five kilometers to get to the point where the bus would pick us up. Annie really needed to rest her knee, so we stopped for a snack. Our timing was tight because once we got to the road, we had only 25 minutes to catch the bus, or face a wait of several hours for the next one. We were going pretty fast considering we had been hiking for several days! As we came around the corner, there was the bus, still there about 10 minutes after it was due to leave. We hustled as fast as we could, and were nearly at the stop when the bus started to move. Our hustle became a run! Thankfully, the driver stopped for us, and as we were paying our fare, I heard a woman up the back say "suerte" ("lucky"). She was right about that!

After a night in El Bolson, Annie and I decided to take a day off at a nearby lake: Lagos Aponte. Annie still had knee issues, and felt a soak in the lake was just what she needed. As for me, I was always ready for a day off after an extended backpacking trip.

We took a bus to the lake early in the day. The only person there was a young man practicing his guitar. A divine place and live music – what a treat. As the day wore on, families came to enjoy the beach. It was fun being a part of regular life as we watched kids and their parents frolic in the water.

The next morning Annie and I split up. She was heading to Baraloche and I was going on to Lago Tricolor. It was difficult and sad to leave my new friend! We had only known each other for a few days, but I felt like she was a sister. We tried to get an ice cream as a farewell, but none of the ice cream parlors were open at 9:00 in the morning! So, a cup of tea and a piece of chocolate cake sufficed as we said goodbye. (A couple of years later, I met up with Annie in Munich and we went hiking in the Alps together!)

The hike to Refugio Cerro Lindo was another steep climbing day. El Bolson is in a valley, with mountains on both sides of it, so the only way to get to those enchanting places was UP! This time I was going from 250 meters all the way up to 1500 meters. But, in my favor, I had all day. Slow and steady got me there.

When I reached the refugio, I asked where the baño (toilet) was. The answer was that it was under construction and all the woods were the baño! Boy, it showed! Argentina and Chile are so proud of their clean water supply, so how could this be happening? I was appalled! On my way down several days later, I met a couple coming the other way. They said they had been here about eight years ago, and the "baño" was under construction then too!

I didn't pay the extra charge to use the kitchen in the refugio. Instead, I found an awesome spot out on some rocks. I had my own running water (hoping it was clean!), a place to set up my stove, and views across the valley. As the sun set behind me and I watched colors change on the mountains, up came the full moon. I'd have missed all this if I had paid to use the kitchen. Way awesome!

Next morning, I set off to see Lago Tricolor. As I climbed up to the Lago, I was back in snow country, with lots of snowfields and melt water.

Not knowing exactly where I would find the lake, I headed a little too far to the right, and thus was treated to a view of the whole El Bolson valley. Now that was a treat I hadn't expected!

I wandered around the rock outcroppings, knowing there was a lake up there somewhere.

Wow!

Awesome!

Spectacular!

What more could I say? This was even more captivating than the pictures on the brochures. I couldn't believe I was lucky enough to be in such a gorgeous spot, on such a lovely day. Life sure felt good! I was basically sitting on cliffs above the lake, and it was impossible to climb down to it. If I could have, I would have collected some lake water and taken it home to put next to the little jar from Three Tarns Pass! Instead, I sat for a couple of hours, reading and loving life in this enchanting spot.

There was another lake up there, and it looked like I could hike to the edge of it. So off I went across the high country. The lake was not hard to get to, but it was surrounded by snow and ice floated on the surface. Wait, wasn't this late summer? I guess I was pretty high up to be greeted by snow and ice like this!

Back down to the refugio, where I gathered up my dinner fixings and went out to my rock dining room. It was so nice out there that I stayed until it was dark and the full moon was high in the sky. When I am in a place like this, I really don't want to leave – I want to hold on to it forever.

My last day was a pleasant downhill hike all the way back to the El Bolson valley. I had fallen in love with this little town in the mountains.

Lake high up in Terra Del Fuego

Paso do La Oveja

Backpacking above Baralocho

Los Lagunos

Glacier Azul and lake

Lago Tricolor

For more photos go to: http://still-going-strong.com

The Pyrenees

● ● ●

... I needed something to pare the fat off my soul, to scare the s**t out of me, to make me grateful, again, for being alive. And I knew, deep and safe, beyond mere intellect that there is nothing like a wilderness journey for rekindling the fires of life. Simplicity is part of it. Cutting the cackle. Transportation reduced to leg - or arm-power, eating irons to one spoon. Such simplicity, together with sweat and silence, amplify the rhythms of any long journey, especially through unknown, untattered territory. And in the end such a journey can restore an understanding of how insignificant you are - and thereby set you free.

Colin Fletcher in <u>River</u>

AUGUST – SEPTEMBER 2012

"500 MILES IS GOOD ENOUGH FOR ME"

Sticking to the highest and most inaccessible trails, the HRP ("Haute Route Pyrénéenne", or Pyrenees High Level Route) crisscrosses the mountainous border between France and Spain. The HRP is one of the most challenging long-distance walking routes in Europe, and at times the trail is difficult to follow and requires careful navigation.

The highest passes on the HRP are often snowy, even in mid-Summer, and the going underfoot can be difficult but the rewards are immeasurable; you visit places that are only accessible on foot, see mountains in their dawn glow and sunset glory, swim in cool mountain lakes and experience the remoteness and true wilderness of the Pyrenees.

Mountainbug.com

MOST HIKERS AND BACKPACKERS HAVE heard about the long trails in the USA. We have three trails that go south to north for several thousand miles, and some backpackers have done all three. I really didn't share their desire to walk that far. As I once told a friend: "A nice 500 mile trail is good enough for me!"

The original idea to do my first long hike came from a dear friend, Skip. We had talked about hiking in the Dolomites, and even though I had plenty of time to do it, my friends couldn't go with me. So Skip handed me a book called The Haute Route of the Pyrenees, written by Ton Joosten, and said, "Take a look at this." I started looking through the book, and before I knew it, I was hooked. I had always wondered if I could do a major long trip, and this one fit the bill.

I believe there is a fine line between being a determined person (positive connotation) and being hard headed (negative connotation). I choose to say that I am determined, and when I get an idea in my head, I have a hard time not doing it. Thus the 500 mile route across the Pyrenees was born for 2012.

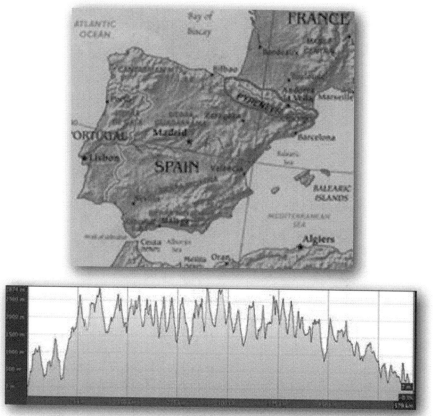

This is the elevation profile from "Backpackinglight.com"
For more detail on maps, go to: http://still-going-strong.com

It looked like a comb! I was going to be doing LOTS of climbing and descending.

When I originally decided to do this trip, I thought I would have hiking partners for at least part of the way. But for one reason or another, each pal ended up with other commitments. As per my modus operandi, I decided that shouldn't deter me from pressing on and planning this trip.

Ton Joosten had backpacked all over the Pyrenees and followed many trails. His book described a trail that basically follows the spine of the Pyrenees all the way from the Atlantic Ocean to the Mediterranean Sea.

I read bits and pieces of the book and was intrigued. I was also a little intimidated. There was lots of elevation gain, long days, and remote foot travel. Would I be able to complete such an arduous hike? Part of my philosophy has always been that if I don't try something, I'll never know if I could have done it. So the answer to the question is: "Start it and see what happens!"

Preparations

I started gathering my gear for this long trek. It was important to pack as light as possible, but there were also some creature comforts I seriously wanted. For goodness sake, I was 66 years old and not a young chicken anymore! For example, when I sleep on the ground, it has to be comfortable or I won't get the rest I need to hike the next day. I also realized I probably would take longer to complete this trail than the book described. I really was going to need a full pack, but one I could carry without dying! So there was a lot of waffling back and forth, deciding on each item of gear.

My book told me which topographical maps I would need, so I went online and found them from a company in England. When they arrived, I discovered just how heavy 12 topo maps were! So, instead of taking entire maps, I made copies of just the sections I would need. The copies were lighter than the actual maps, but were still heavy – however, there was no way I could complete the trail without them. As I finished with each one, I could dispose of it - in a responsible manner of course.

I had two rather important pieces of gear to add to my equipment: A GPS and a SPOT locator beacon. My niece's husband had ordered them for me at cost price, so it wasn't too expensive, and I was really excited to have this new technology in my bag of tricks. I put way-points on the GPS so I could see where the trail went. And, after all those years of renting a locator beacon in New Zealand and Australia, I finally had my own. It was much lighter and smaller than the rental ones!

Despite my excitement, concerns kept cropping up. It looked like a hard route. Would I be able to follow the trail? I am not very proficient in Spanish, and even less so in French. Would the language barrier be a factor? What about food? Would I be able to resupply myself? What about being a solo female hiker? And an older one, at that? Would I be safe? These questions kept popping up in my mind, usually at 3:00am! At some point, I just had to let go of all that nonsense. I was going! No turning back. I set a date for August and September, and started telling all my friends. That made it a little more real to me.

My Buddy Takes Me There

Being the way I am i.e. the cheapest person on the planet, I found a wonderfully inexpensive way to get to Spain. My good friend, Tom, was a retired Delta pilot. As part of Tom's retirement package, he received "buddy passes", which he offered to let me use. I gratefully accepted his kind offer, and that cut my travel costs by half.

To use a buddy pass you must fly stand-by. That means you only fly if there are empty seats after the plane is boarded. It is a bit of an unknown as to whether you will get on the plane or not, but as I did not have a set schedule, it was no problem if I had to wait a day or two for a flight.

At 6:00am, on July 31, 2012, I took the bus to Denver International and got on a flight to New York just fine....followed by an 18 hour layover at JFK! I managed to entertain myself, and by 6:00pm the following day, I was waiting at the gate hoping to get on the flight to Barcelona. After they boarded the plane, I heard my name being called! I had a seat! And, guess what??? My seat was in First Class!!

I had decided to fly to Barcelona, on the Mediterranean coast, even though my route was to start on the Atlantic side of the Pyrenees. When I arrived in Barcelona, I booked a train ticket to Irun, the Spanish town closest to Hendaye – the start of my route.

I had a few hours to tour Barcelona before my train, but I was too wiped out from not enough sleep. Besides, Barcelona was pretty hot. So, I found a cool spot in the shade and took a quick siesta. For my safety and security, I had my passport, credit card and cash in a bag sewn inside my pants, so I could relax enough to get a nap.

The train finally got to Irun about 10:30pm. I had no idea what kind of town Irun was, but I was hoping there might be a cheap hotel or hostel near the station. There wasn't, so I started walking around the town. I soon decided this was not a good thing to be doing at 11:00pm, so I asked a taxi driver to take me to a small hotel or hostel. Now remember, I was in Spain and my Spanish is marginal at best. Even though the communication was a bit shabby, I did get my point across and he took me to a great hostel.

On The Right Track…I Think?

The next day, I crossed the border into France. When I reached the beach at Hendaye, I plopped my pack in the sand, took off my boots and socks and waded out into the Atlantic Ocean. I took a couple of photos of my feet in the water and thought, "Now my trip is REALLY starting!" It was August 3rd, and I headed through the town by following the red and white marks painted on walls and lamp posts.

There are three main routes across The Pyrenees from the Atlantic to the Mediterranean: The GR 10, the GR11, and the HRP (Haute Route Pyrénéenne). My book described the HRP and that was my main route. Sometimes, though, the HRP joined the GR10 or GR11, and that was the way this trek was starting. The nice part of overlapping with one of the GR trails was that the trail markings were easier to see.

However, after only 20 minutes, I lost the route! I asked for directions from people on the street, showing them my route in the book, and finally found my way out of town. Little did I realize, this would end up being a regular occurrence. Most of the times I lost the trail, I was in a city! The little red and white marks took me along just fine...that was, until they disappeared, leaving me to fumble my way through the tiny streets.

I was finally out of town, and following the route. It was mostly along roads for this first part of the trip. I was hot, I was tired, and I had already run out of water. This was not starting well. I walked up a hill on the edge of a paved road and thought I heard running water. Hmmm... ok. I investigated, and saw water coming out of a pipe from somewhere under the road. The pipe was part of a cement block, and the water looked clean. Even so, I knew it probably wasn't the best place to get water, so I got out my SteriPEN, which purifies water with ultraviolet light. I was at least happy that I had some water, and hopefully it wouldn't make me sick!

It was now getting rather late – almost 6:00pm. I was walking along roads, and even though I was following what the book described, I couldn't see any place that I considered appropriate for camping. As I was going up a hill into the village of Biriatou, I saw a sign that pointed two ways. It said the village was to the left, but if you went to the village by taking the right fork, there were shops and restaurants. I decided I should find a restaurant, have a good dinner, and then work out what to do.

As I came around the bend, not only was there a restaurant, but there was a hotel. I was not at all concerned about how much it would cost; I had found a home for the night. It felt really good to take my pack off my back and have a long soak in the bathtub. My muscles said "thank you!"

Dinner was a total gourmet experience. I ordered lamb (my favorite) that came with an appetizer - a single scallop on a fancy plate – plus soup, and crème brulée for desert. I thought I had died and gone to heaven!! I knew I would pay big money for this, but at that point, I really didn't care!

After a good night's sleep, I felt much better. Breakfast was another gourmet meal, which got my day off to a great start. Of course the bill was outrageous for a night's stay, but like I said, it was totally worth it. I just had to remember that not all nights could, or would, be like this.

Ton Joosten's book was not easy to follow. Quite a few of the landmarks he had listed were no longer there. The book was written in 2003, and this was 2012. A lot can change in nine years. Fortunately, he was wrong about not being able to buy food on a Sunday, and I found several cafés were open. It was a treat to stop for coffee and a snack.

I got to Col de Lizuniaga late afternoon. It had taken two days to get there; the book said it should take one day. Just as well I had given myself 60 days to complete the route, and not the 42 days listed in the book. When I checked my GPS, I saw I had walked 20 miles from the beach at Hendaye. So this book would have me doing 20-mile days? I don't think so...

The next few days took me through the Basque region of Spain. The track went from village to village, sometimes on a dirt trail but mostly along a paved road. When it left the dirt track, there were some good markings, but often it was very confusing. I was beginning to wonder about this trek!

I was going up and down over several "Col's. Sometimes, the passes were called "Puertos" and sometimes "Cols"! Puerto is the Spanish name for a pass (it means door) and Col is the French name. By the way, you'll also notice that sometimes I stay in a "refuge" one night, and a "refugio" the next night. A refuge is the French name for a place of shelter...and a refugio is the Spanish word for it. In the Pyrenees, where I'd cross from France to Spain, and vice versa, quite often, the change from refuge to refugio would be frequent. Confused much?!

After several days, I finally got to Col de Roncevaux. From this col, there was a road down to the village of Roncesvalles, where my trail crossed the trail of the Camino de Santiago, the famous pilgrimage. It was overrun with pilgrims! I would rather camp than spend the night in Roncesvalles, but I needed batteries for my GPS. Rather than stay around Roncesvalles, I hitched to Valcarlos. I found a hotel room and a shop where I could buy batteries. While I had a beer, I started re-evaluating my route.

I had been following the Haute Route for five days now, but I was not even in the mountains yet! At this rate, it seemed it would take me years to get to the Mediterranean. I felt like I was wearing myself out walking on these roads. I needed mountains! So I read the route descriptions for the next few days and discovered that the little town of Lescun marked the start of the higher mountain trail. It took a full day of bus and train travel to get to Lescun, but one look at the mountains and I was a much happier hiker!

Day Seven, I hiked up, up, up to Col de Pau. It took me hours to climb this trail, and as I got to the Col, there was an older couple with their grandchildren! The kids, who were about four or five years old, were dancing around singing little songs. I was amazed these children had climbed up here and were having such a great time. When the grandparents showed me the way they were planning on going down, I was even more amazed. They were totally taking the little kids "off trail".

That afternoon I hiked to the Refuge d'Arlet. When I got there, I asked the hut keeper if it would be possible to join the table for dinner. He looked at me and said, "Just one? You?" He pointed to a spot at a table and said to sit there at 7:00pm. I was so happy I wanted to hug him.

I went out, set up my tent and organized my gear. Then I went down to the lake to splash water on my dirty body. At 7:00pm I was in the refuge, enjoying a delicious meal with 50 other people! At my table was another older lady who had hiked to the refuge with her great nephew. He spoke a little English and we could communicate, but most of the people in the refuge were French and didn't speak English.

The next morning, the trail went down to the very bottom of the valley, and then up the other side. This would be the pattern for this hike across the Pyrenees. The trail was a little exposed in parts, and there was even a place where I had to climb a ladder. The last part of this steep trail was a bit of hand and foot climbing, but it opened out to a lovely spot. I stopped and looked down over a beautiful lake below. I met some hikers from Ireland and a couple of girls from Holland who came over the pass while I was stopped.

As I got down to the lake, the Dutch girls, Sonna and Eline, were having a swim. Of course they had brought bathing suits, which was definitely not on my gear list. I am not a lover of swimming in cold water, but I did get in as it felt great to get some of the sweat and salt off my body. I then lay on a big rock to warm up and dry off. We started up a conversation and I found out that Sonna and Eline were going on to Candanchú. That was my destination too, but I had decided this lake would be a wonderful place to spend the night. There was a herd of horses and a few sheep wandering around, but there was also a nice, flat place for my tent. So the girls went on while I stayed at the lake.

A couple of people came up from the direction I would be going the next day. They were day hikers. One young lady came by to talk to me. When I told her I was going to camp here, she was amazed. She asked a couple of times if I was going to camp all by myself! I guess being solo is unusual not only in the United States, South America, and New Zealand, but also all over Europe.

I had a wonderful bivouac that evening. Just me and the horses and the sheep. Each of those horses and sheep had a bell around their necks. The "donging" of their bells went on all night long, but I guess I considered that music to my ears, because I slept great.

Next morning, off I went - down, down, down, only to find out that I had gone down the wrong drainage. I had to climb over a ridge to get back on my route and the road to the pass. I hitched until a nice lady finally picked me up. She was on her way to the top of the pass to pick up her husband. After picking him up, they decided to drive me down to the village of Candanchú and show me their favorite hotel. Sounded good to me! So they dropped me off, and I went in and booked a room.

After finding my room, I reserved a place for dinner. Then I headed out to see if there was a shop to buy batteries. I loved my GPS, but it used a lot of batteries. As I was walking out the driveway, there were Sonna and Eline, my Dutch friends who had been swimming in the lake. We hugged and laughed about all of us ending up in the same hotel, and we agreed to have dinner together. Then I wandered around the little shops (not much here!) and did get some batteries – little did I know that finding batteries would be an on-going issue for me.

Sonna and Eline and I compared stories over dinner. Like me, they had got totally lost trying to get to Candanchú. They ended up in the dark, but as they did not have full packs with a tent, they didn't have the option of camping for the night. Finally they came upon some hunters who gave them a ride into Candanchú. That made me feel a little better about my misdirected route. We also realized that we were planning the same route for the next day. They were not hiking the whole Haute Route.

Instead, they were doing five days of backpacking, and then to the beach for the rest of their holiday.

So, up we went to the ski area. I met some other girls on the bus; one was sick, so I gave her my seat in the front of the bus. Little did I know that, a couple of days later, I would end up hiking and staying with these young women. The chairlift was great, and cost only five euros. It took me up through the clouds and into clear blue skies. Once at the top, they gave me two euros back. A strange system!

Sonna and Eline had arranged to stay in Refuge d'Ayous, but I preferred to eat in the refuge and sleep out in my tent. The tenting area was down by the lake, so I went and set up and had a nice relaxing hour before dinner. Across the lake there was a spectacular view of Pic du Midi d'Ossau. The next morning, Sonna and Eline headed back to Candanchú and I headed off on my Haute Route. I was yet to meet anyone doing the whole Haute Route, and I hadn't found a single American hiker.

My next destination was Refuge d'Arrémoulit. In the description of that day's hike there was a spot that sounded a bit tricky. It was called the "Passage d'Orteig" and the book described it as:

"...not too difficult, but impressive. It can be awkward for those who suffer from vertigo and dangerous in bad weather... Climb steeply above a deep abyss and finally, past the Passage d'Orteig, walk east in a chaos of boulders ..."

The book gave me an option of walking down to a lake, and then up the other side to get to the refuge. The use of the word "abyss" didn't exactly ease my worries! When I got near the passage, I decided to at least take a look. There were three Spanish guys on the trail, and they said it wasn't too bad. At least, I think that's what they said. They were speaking Spanish!

They offered me some wine from their "bota bag". (I sure understood that!) I thought a sip of wine before this tricky trail might settle my nerves. After my sip, and not wanting to go all the way down to the lake and back up again, I pressed ahead and committed to the Passage d'Orteig. There were cables bolted to the rocks that I could hold on to. That gave me a sense of security. Without letting my brain go to the place of nervousness, I just took one step after another and really focused on what I was doing. There was a little section where I had to climb about 10 feet, and I was definitely pulling on the cable to get me up. But past that spot, I felt more comfortable. And the next thing I knew, I had done the Passage d'Orteig. Relieved? You bet!

The trail was a bit sketchy over the top of this little pass. It really was a chaos of boulders, but soon I could look down and see the Refuge d'Arrémoulit. Because of all the boulders, there weren't many campsites, so I hiked down to a lake below the refuge and found a tiny level spot – it was barely the size of my tent.

The girls from the bus were in the hut at dinner time. As I got to know them, I found out they were teachers from Austria, Germany and Spain (Ursula, Barbara, and Pipi). They could speak very good English and it was a joy to talk with them. They also spoke excellent Spanish as Ursula and Barbara taught that language. It was fun comparing experiences on the Passage d'Orteig. Ursula had been all the way down to the lake and back up. They were only hiking another couple of days then had to go home. They were very interested in me, and wanted to hear about my route. They were traveling lighter than I was, since they weren't carrying camping gear. I was beginning to realize that it was quite unusual for anyone to carry camping gear up here.

The next morning's trail headed up through boulders to the pass. Ursula, Barbara and Yuri were following me, and at the top, they thanked me for leading them. I thought that was pretty funny! Then, I followed them down the other side! It was a better trail on the way down to the next refuge – Refuge Respomuso. It was only 1:00pm, and a bit early to stop, but a big storm was expected, so I thought I would make a reservation, and sleep indoors that night. The hut keeper said he would know about 3:00pm if I could have a bed. Sure enough, at 3:00pm, he put my name into a slot with a bed number. And joy of joys, this refugio had hot showers! By 5:00pm it was pouring, so I had made the right decision to stay.

I had been sleeping in my tent for a couple of weeks now, so to sleep in a bed was a big transition for me. The room was stuffy and noisy. I opened a window, but someone else closed it. And, the smoke alarm on the ceiling was flashing in my face! I paid extra for this? At least I was dry inside, while it stormed outside. I knew I wouldn't be getting much sleep if I was in my tent in that storm.

The next morning, my trail lapped onto the GR 11. After about one hour, I met up with several groups who had camped out. One couple, Tim and Laura, were from England, and I had met them when we camped next to Refuge d'Ayous. Not only did they survive the cold night but when we got to a high mountain lake they went swimming! Yikes! (Two years later I visited them in Bath, England.)

Later that day, I met a delightful French couple who didn't speak any English. It would have been great fun to talk with these lovely people. But, alas, my brain doesn't retain different languages, so in depth discussions just don't happen. I always carried my book on the Haute Route in my front packs, and I pulled it out to show my route. I think heard every possible exclamation in French and Spanish! I guess I am an anomaly in any country!

This French couple also wanted to know how heavy my pack was. So I took off my pack and the man lifted it. I may not have understood all he said, but he definitely said it was too heavy!

When I got down to Wallen, there was Marixa and Oriel, a Barcelona couple who had been "leap frogging" with me. Marixa and Oriel said they were going to the next lake to camp. It was only 3:30pm so I ate an omelet at Wallen Refuge and followed them up to the lake.

(A funny thing to add about my new Spanish friends, Marixa and Oriel. When I was finished with the whole Haute Route, I had dinner with them in Barcelona. After a couple of beers, they told me they had nicknamed me "The Ant" when I was on the trail, because I just kept coming. Every time they would stop to rest, I would catch up with them. So then they started calling me "The Bionic Ant"!)

That evening while we were camping, Marixa, Oriel and I talked about the weight of my pack. I said that when I could get to a post office, I would mail some things home. We looked at each piece of my gear and tried to figure what I could send. One item was my SteriPEN, which purifies water. Oriel said it was too heavy and that I should carry iodine drops instead. They had enough tablets to get through their hike, so he kindly gave me their bottle of iodine to use for the rest of my trip.

The next morning, I said goodbye to Marixa and Oriel and set off towards the next refuge - Refuge Oulettes. I had three passes to go over. The first was pretty straight forward, but there was a large cirque to go around to get to the next pass. It reminded me of Yule Pass back home in Crested Butte, and the Paso de Ovejas in South America. After that pass, it was a long way down to Refuge Oulettes, in front of a mountain called the Vignemale.

All winter in Crested Butte, as I had pored over my book on the Pyrenees, I kept seeing a photo of tents in front of Vignemale's North Face. One of my mantras was: "I want to see my tent in that spot!" That day when I got to "that spot", it was too early to stop for the day and camp. So I dug down into my pack and pulled out my tent. I then set it up and took photos of it with the mountain behind it! After the photo session, I took the tent back down, and repacked my pack!

I got to Refuge Oulettes in good time. Since it was still too early to stop, I headed on to the next refuge. It was not a fun climb to the pass as my back was really bothering me. At the top, I pulled out my mini-masseuse and when I put it on my back muscles, I had almost instant relief. Whew, that thing just paid for itself! I was NOT sending that home!

From the top of the pass, it was a relatively gentle hike down to Refuge Bayssellance. This refuge is the highest of all the huts in the Pyrenees. It was good to be there after climbing three passes that day, and I was happy to camp in my tent again, where it was cool and quiet.

The next day was mostly downhill to Gavarnie, where I had a reservation at a local refuge. I had already decided that I would take a day off in Gavarnie and on Monday morning I would send a box home with anything I absolutely didn't need for the rest of the trip.

On Sunday morning, I redistributed my pack, did laundry, and had a very relaxing day wandering around Gavarnie. I felt right at home since Gavarnie is a ski town and the Cirque de Gavarnie is a beautiful set of mountains.

On Monday morning, I showed up at the post office to mail some of my stuff home. I had been very brutal with what could, and couldn't, stay in my pack. Unfortunately, the postal lady only spoke French, so our communications were a bit awkward. When I told her I needed a box to mail things home, she wouldn't give me one from the shelf. I finally figured that those boxes were only for mailing inside France. So I asked if she had any other boxes, and she went to the back room and got one. Then she used scotch tape to put the box together. I don't know much about the

French postal service, but scotch tape holding a box together in the USA probably wouldn't make it!

I put my things in the box, and the postal lady used another 15 short pieces of tape to close it. Then she put it on the scale and started shaking her head. She looked back and forth between her computer and my box, and got more and more irritated with me for not understanding. Finally she gave the box to me, and said "NO"! I couldn't figure out why she wouldn't send it!

A lady at the nearby visitors' center overheard this encounter, and told me the box was too heavy! It was only about seven pounds, so I was really surprised. Much to her chagrin, I asked the postal lady for a second box. With a large sigh and a look to kill, she went into the back room and got another box. Then out came the scotch tape again...

I divided my items into two boxes, but now they were loose and rattling around – not a good way to ship things. I was beginning to doubt if these items would ever get home. But, mentally and physically, I was desperate. I didn't want to throw this stuff in the trash, but I was definitely not carrying it any further. So both boxes went back to the mail counter. She weighed them, and then started telling me about something else she was having a problem with. I was clueless, so the visitor center lady again came to translate. The postal clerk was telling me the cost to mail the boxes – and it was more than rather expensive.

"I DON"T CARE! Even if it costs me hundreds of dollars, just SEND THEM!"

Very begrudgingly, the clerk took my money. I had just spent way too much to send this stuff home (about 50 euros), and it probably wouldn't even make it. (Believe it or not, both boxes DID make it all the way to

Crested Butte. Joni said they looked like they had been through the Super Bowl, but they were in one piece!)

I was finally ready to leave Gavarnie, albeit with a bit of a sour taste in my mouth thanks to the postal lady. It was about 10:30am as I walked through town to the trailhead. I stopped at the ATM. After spending all that money at the post office, I needed to replenish my cash! Finally, I was on the trail again after my first day off.

It was up, up, up to the pass, and then down, down, down on the other side. This is pretty much what I did for 55 days. Going up, then going down! While I was hiking down, I met a very cute French runner. I was impressed that he was running these trails, and he was just impressed that I was hiking all the way across the Pyrenees.

My book, map and GPS showed a lake almost at the bottom of this valley so I planned that as my next camping spot. When I got there though, the terrain was steep and rocky and there was no level place to put my tent. The route from there went down about five kilometers, on a paved road to the little town of Héas. I stopped in the parking lot to ask a couple if this actually was the road to Héas. They told me it was and, if I would like, they could give me a ride down to the town. I gladly accepted their kind offer! They dropped me at a campground in that remote village.

I was happy to have a place to pitch my tent, and happier still after a hot shower. Then I sat on the patio for dinner. Once again, I had a bit of a communication problem with the waitress, until a young lady a couple of tables over asked if I needed any translation help. She was an AMERICAN! The first American I had seen on this whole trip! So I changed tables and joined her. Her name was Helen and she was, from all places, Denver. Yes, both of us were from Colorado, and both of us were solo backpacking. She was not doing the same route as mine, but shorter three or four day trips through the mountains. We had a great time sharing stories and talking about the Pyrenees.

At the end of the meal, I paid in Euros and Helen tried to pay with her credit card. Unfortunately, her card wouldn't work in the machine the waitress had. They tried several times to make it work, all to no avail. So I offered to pay for her meal with Euros and she agreed to reimburse me with American Dollars. Helen and I made plans to meet for breakfast before we headed off in different directions.

I had a big climb the next day of 1100 meters (that's about 3,300 feet). Along the way, I saw a little religious memorial with a story etched on the stone above it. A French couple came by while I was there and translated it for me. And then, while we were still there, along came the cute runner I had met yesterday! He totally recognized me, and we laughed about seeing each other again.

The next section was an amazing part of the hike. The trail went right next to huge cliffs and around rocks and scree to a large shelf, which had been almost impossible to see. That was where the Refuge de Barroude was located. There was even a lake there – a truly wonderful spot. I got there about 6:00pm, but still in time to put my name in the pot for dinner and breakfast. And, of course, to have a beer before I set up my tent! It was a delicious dinner, complete with tiramisu for dessert.

Several days later, I was climbing up, yet again, to a pass. I still had a long way to the top when I met a German boy. He was doing the Haute Route – FINALLY I had met someone else doing it! He had a box strapped to the back of his pack, and when I asked him about it, he said the box had his old boots in it. He did not want to throw them away. Instead, he wanted to mail them home! (Does this sound familiar?) He was going to go down a different drainage than me because he wanted to get to a post office before the weekend.

At the top of that pass was a non-staffed hut. It was the first one I had seen that was not locked, so I was excited to stay in it. I discovered that it was possible to drive to this spot. There was a lake about a quarter of a mile down that looked like a favorite fishing area. Some people were having a late lunch at the hut, but they weren't spending the night, so I found a "mattress" upstairs and claimed my spot for the evening. Then I grabbed a snack and my Kindle, and went out to sit on the rocks above the lake.

I was having a relaxing time watching other people hike down to the water, including a gentleman who was going to do some fishing. I then heard a car pull up, but I couldn't see it over the little hill. Next thing I knew, two policemen were coming down toward me. Sacré bleu!

Of course, they only spoke French, so there were communication issues again. I finally figured out they were looking for a single female hiker who had called in that she had broken her leg. As I was a single female hiker, they wanted to be sure it wasn't me. I told them it wasn't...my leg was just fine, and unbroken. But thank you, all the same!

As it was getting a little late, I broke out my bread, cheese and salami and sat in the hut eating. At times like this, it would have been really nice to still have my stove to fix a hot drink...but that had been mailed home from Gavarnie! The fisherman came in and luckily he spoke some English. He was spending the night there also. He chose a mattress on the other side of the room, and we both went to bed relatively early.

About midnight, another car drove up. It was a family and they decided it was a good time to fix their supper, and in the process, make a racket right below us. I didn't have a handle on the French language, so I didn't feel like I could do much about it. But my fisherman friend wasn't having any of it. He walked down the stairs and read the family "the riot act" in French! They sure were quiet diners after that! Later, they were just as quiet coming up into the sleeping area. In the morning, I was on my way before anyone else was even awake, so I never got to see France's noisiest family!

My route this day would take me up to a very high pass. The book suggested I ask at the Refugio de Viados about the conditions. When I did, they said I would need an ice axe and crampons for the high route. Ice axe?? CRAMPONS??? Oofta! I guessed I'd be taking the lower route…

As I started out from Viados, I met two hikers coming down the trail. When I asked them about the routes ahead of me, they said they had just come over the high route. They reported there was NO snow or glaciers to cross, so back to plan A – the high route!

It was tough going, with scree and boulders and hardpan dirt up a gully. This route might get interesting! Just before the pass, I noticed a little sheltered rock spot. I went on up to the pass, but came back and camped by the sheltered rocks. It was pretty cloudy and starting to rain, and as I looked out before dark, there was an Izard (a Pyrenean Chamois) looking right back at me. I love being on the high routes!

The next day, my trail went down to La Soula. The guy at the refuge there was very sweet. I ordered a ham and cheese sandwich to go, and he gave me extra bread and a piece of local cheese. While I was eating, the clouds moved in. I thought I'd hike out of them as I went higher, but it just got worse. So up I went, encountering lots of switchbacks. The trail was easy to see, which was good, as I was definitely in the clouds!

I met two French girls, Annabelle and Flo, at the dam. They had decided to camp there, but I thought I would like to go on to the lakes. But, it was so socked in, and the trail looked so marginal, that I backtracked and camped by the dam with Annabelle and Flo. Anabelle was doing the

Haute Route too. She had friends and family joining her along the way. They were really short on water, but I had enough to share with them. Crisis averted!

The next morning was clear. I followed Anabelle and Flo for a while, then let them blast ahead. I climbed to the next lakes and then a col between two big peaks. I think Anabelle and Flo were going to climb those peaks. At lunch, I spread out my wet tent to dry while I ate, before setting off again. Up and over the next pass I went, and then around and around and around before seeing the next refuge - Refuge du Portillon. There was a level spot next to the refuge where I could camp, and each individual camping section was surrounded by small rock walls. Later, Annabelle and Flo came and camped near me.

The next morning, Anabelle and Flo left the refuge just before me. I was worried about the pass, and, of course, I lost the trail first thing and had to shimmy up a crack. It was a nerve wracking way to start the day. Anabelle and Flo also lost the trail, and went up the wrong side of the drainage. Then they headed over to where I was, and we met up. The three of us went up the sketchy trail on the left of the glacier by Col Inferior de Literole. The top of the trail was even scarier! For all this, I followed them. Once again the Universe had provided people to be with me during a sketchy section! The other side, typically, didn't seem as bad as I had been told. Anabelle and Flo watched me go down. They weren't treated to the prettiest of descents, and I slipped just a bit, but I made it fine.

A couple of days later though, I came to the most difficult, scary, dangerous down-climb of the whole trip. My guardian angels must have been out to lunch, because no one showed up and I was definitely on my own. I had just climbed to the Tuc (Peak) de Mulleres at 3010 meters. Just below that was the Col (Pass) de Mulleres. I was looking down – straight down – a very steep rock wall and boulder field. It was only about 50 meters to the boulder field, but there was no safe or easy way down. I had to use some pretty marginal hand holds and foot holds. I probably looked at it longer than I should have, because I was getting more and more nervous. Going back wasn't an option. I needed to "suck it up" and start down. That I did! Each foot hold and hand hold needed to be checked before I put my weight on it. It took about an hour to go 50 meters (that's only 150 feet), but slow and steady did the trick. I eventually worked my way down till I was in the boulder field. WHEW! I was shaking from the concentration and effort but I was DOWN!

A bit further on, I met a young man on the trail who was out of water, so once again I shared what water I had. That night I found a great spot near a stream to camp, but there was a downside - hundreds of flies!!

It never stopped raining the following day. I was glad I had done the Col de Mulleres the day before. When I got to the Refuge de la Restanca, it was still foggy and cloudy. My spirits were lifted when I saw Anabelle and her mom! (By this stage, Flo had gone on home) We had a great chat, and then I enjoyed a hot shower. Joe, the young man I had given water to then arrived, and bought me a beer. We had dinner with six of us HRP adventurers – Andie and Claire (French), Joe (Belgium), Anabelle and Mom (French) and me. Since I had been sharing water with these new friends, they all insisted on buying me beers. I had three beers - way over my limit!

Another day, another period of bad weather. This time it was cold and windy. I went straight up from Restanca, and it got windier and windier as I went higher and higher. This was a "no map" day, so I paid close attention to my book and the GPS. I got down to a road and hitchhiked into Salardú. My friend, Xavi from Crested Butte, knew someone running the local refuge, so I chose to stay there for my next day off.

It was September 2. I had been on the trail for a month. The weather in the high mountains was beginning to change. Cooler temperatures, more clouds. It felt like fall.

The next morning, as I hiked out of Salardú, the weather deteriorated as I went. I got up to some lakes and set up camp early. It was a long time in the tent!

The next night, I found an unstaffed refugio, and a lovely Spanish couple sharing it with me. They had been out picking raspberries and we ate them by the spoonful. Since the weather was so icky, I decided to hike down from the high mountains and hitch to Alós d'Isil, Llavorsi, and then Tavascan. In the morning, the mountain tops where I had been were covered with snow. I had made a good choice in deciding to come down from up there!

Xavi had another friend with a hostel in Tavascan. It was a picturesque yet tiny town. I decided to take another day off while I waited for the weather to clear. It was another good choice, because the following day dawned with sunny skies. After a five kilometer walk on a dirt road, the trail went up…and up some more…and up even more! Again, I got to a fun unstaffed refugio in the high country called Cinquantenaire. It looked like a little orange Christmas package from afar.

It was all downhill to start the next day, before I went along a stream at the bottom. I stopped at Refugio de Vall Ferrera and had an incredibly delicious sandwich and coffee to celebrate crossing the 300 mile mark on my GPS. I got another sandwich to go and started hiking up to Pla de Boet. Along the way I saw a family that had been in Tavascan, and they recognized me. After a brief chat, I headed back up, over the pass, before stopping at a stunning lake – Etang de la Soucarrane. This was probably my favorite camping spot of the whole trip. Could that be because I love high mountain lakes?

The following day, there was an adventure race on my route, and I cheered them on as they came past me. The race involved biking and running, and I kept bumping into some of them during the day. It was an amazing course! My personal course took me up to Port de Rat, where I crossed over into Andorra.

At the top of the pass, I talked to the race marshal before heading down to a ski area. The restaurant was open and I enjoyed a hearty lunch of chicken, hamburger, salad, fries, and coffee! After this feast, I started up the trail. Thunder and lightning was in the air, so I camped early.

The next morning, it was a fantastic walk down; first on ski slopes, and then by a stream on an "old road". I got to El Serrat, where the restaurant was able to satisfy my appetite, this time with coffee, croissant, ham and cheese and bread. I had a hard time finding the trail out of town and had to go back and ask directions. I finally found the trail, but the refuge was under construction, so I stopped, put my feet up, and napped. I also laid out my tent to dry. As I headed up to the next pass, a thunderstorm chased me into the tent before I could get there.

It was a gorgeous, clear morning as I packed and headed up the pass. At one point on the trail, I sneezed and it was like the ground exploded! I had scared about 40 Izards. In Colorado we have lots of deer and elk in the high country – here they have Izards, a type of goat antelope, about the size of small deer. Believe me, they scared me as much as I scared them! It was quite a sight to see them running through those high mountains.

Up and over the first pass I went, and down the other side. The refuge my book described was closed up tight, and looked like it had been that way for several years. Never mind. I found a nice picnic area further on to camp in and had the place to myself – fresh water and all!

350 miles registered! Up to the next refuge, where I got a sandwich and coffee. I met a French couple in their seventies. See…there's no age limit in this game! They followed me over the first pass, but then went off in another direction. I went over a second pass (Col de l'Albe), out of

Andorra and back into France. Up and down until thunderstorms made me set up my camp for the night.

For my third day off, I stopped in 'Hospitalet du Andorra and took a train into Toulouse. I needed to get to an outdoor equipment store to buy repair tape for my sleeping pad, and a few more maps. My GPS didn't have maps downloaded for the end of the trail, and I needed better paper maps than I currently had.

On the trail again, and I was following the red and white stripes of the GR10. This made me smile! The route finding on the Haute Route had been rather difficult at times, so I had decided to do the last 140 miles on the GR10 and GR 11. In several places they were the same trail anyway.

I stopped at Bésines and had a sandwich and wine. The "Shepard's Hut" at Rouzet was marked on the map but it was small and had no bunks so I decided to camp above it. The next day, I decided to take the variant listed in the book. It was up to the pass on an eroded path, then down to a huge lake – Bouillouses. There, I had an awesome lunch. I did like the idea of backpacking in the Pyrenees and stopping for lunch with a beer or glass of wine. How very civilized!

I hiked down past three lakes, and onto the GR 11 again. As I was going down, I met a mountain biker coming up. His name was Martin, a German who had been living in Barcelona for the last 15 years. He was fascinated with my route through the mountains. I camped in the valley, and Martin stopped on his way back down. We sat and talked some more, until I was shivering so much I had to dive into my tent.

My trail switched from the GR 11 to the GR 10 and went down to Super Bolquère, a ski area, before going back up to Col de la Perche. I was pretty slim on food so I was hoping to find some sort of shop to resupply. Luckily, in the last little town there was a butcher shop, and a small bakery/grocery...both open, even though it was Sunday. Then I went down to Planes, and got a room and board, and two beers, for a total of 37 Euros. How good was that?

The next morning, I hiked up and out of Planes, and ended my day at La Caranca Refuge. At the refuge, I met Joan (pronounced John) who was closer to my own age. We exchanged info and he said he wanted me to go and see him in Barcelona when I was finished. That made five people I now had to go and see when I hit Barcelona!

Another milestone to celebrate the next day – I passed 400 miles. In doing so, I ended up in the tiny commune of Mantet. It was early but I decided to stop because clouds were pouring over the pass. I found a room in a hostel for 35 Euros. It was nice to have a shower and a hearty dinner while it was stormy outside. Another couple staying at the hostel shared the kitchen with me. The lady spoke English so she was a great translator.

Sunny weather greeted me the next morning as I made my way over Col de Mantet. The trail went down to the little hamlet of Py. I could see gardens full of flowers and vegetables. They were so green and alive. Coming over the Col de Mantet seemed like a real transition from mountain villages and country, to more of a Mediterranean environment. I was getting closer...less than 100 miles to go!

A couple of days later, at the Refuge Marsalli, I met Nues and Andre who also lived in Barcelona. They were planning on climbing the Peak du Canigou. It is a landmark for people living in Catalonia, and every Catalonian thinks they should climb it! Nues thought I should climb it too. I had said the whole way that my goal was to hike this trail, not to climb peaks. But when I put my pack on, it felt really good and I started thinking about climbing that last peak. So, when I got to the junction, I said, "Yes. Let's climb!"

I took the trail that headed up the valley to the mountain. The last section was half an hour of hand over hand climbing. It was a little scary, but I went slowly and carefully. Nues was on top too, along with about 30 people. This was just like being on a Colorado 14er! I added Nues to my ever-growing list of people to see when I got to Barcelona.

As I worked my way to Mines de Batére, I met two guys doing the Haute Route. One was going my way, and the other was heading in the opposite direction. I booked a dorm bed and, proving this hike wasn't all glitz and glamor, I did some laundry!

I woke up above the clouds. Then, I hiked down into them. It was the first day of pig season, with lots of orange-clad hunters and their dogs all over the place. It was a bit nerve wracking with all the barking and shooting going on. I was pleased to get away from there.

The trail went right through the town of Amalie. I needed to buy even more batteries, go to the bank, and get food. Then, I asked at the info desk for directions to my trail and the lady sent me up the wrong drainage! I had a big climb tomorrow, so I wasn't happy about the extra mileage that day.

The next day was – you guessed it - up, up, up. The sky closed in as I approached the top. I actually couldn't tell if I was at the top or not. The area didn't match the description in the book, so I wandered among the rocks looking for landmarks. When I didn't find them, I headed down the way I came until I got back on the GR 10. I don't like wandering around in the fog not knowing where I am going. It was good to finally see some trail markings!

I found an unstaffed refuge at Salinas. It was very dark and smelled like smoke, but at least it was out of the weather. The wind blew all night and there were tons of stars. All the while, I was comfy and warm. I lay there thinking to myself that I would miss these special mountain places.

For the next few days, the trail was lined by blackberries, so I was eating fresh fruit all along the way. My feet were tired as I walked into Le Perthus after doing 15 miles. The refuge was still a long way up the trail, and with my aching feet, going there wasn't an option. So I booked a room in the only open hotel and slept like a log.

From Le Perthus, I got to Refuge d'Olette just before lunchtime. I ordered a sandwich and coffee and talked with a nice British guy who spent most of his time in Laroque-des-Albères. He was my age (67), and would often climb up to the refuge with his dogs. Then, as I came out of the refuge, I saw a most welcome sight. A sign for Banyuls-sur-Mer – it was my finishing point, and it was just eight hours away!

I just about shouted for joy! I was almost there!!!! I had been looking at the name Banyuls-sur-Mer for a year, ever since I started the planning this trip. I had told people I was hiking from Hendaye to Banyuls-sur-Mer. And now, here was the sign telling me I was just hours away.

Yes, Yes, YES!

There was still some work to do, including a mainly uphill hike over the next pass. It was pretty windy, so at about 5:00pm, when I had already done 11 miles for the day, I found a place where I could camp. My GPS showed 495 miles. I would pass 500 miles tomorrow. And tomorrow, I would also reach Banyuls-sur-Mer!

You'd think perfect weather would greet me on this momentous day. Actually, it was really windy in the morning. My little camp in the woods had been great, but even so, the wind had pulled out the bottom stake of my tent. But I didn't have far to go. Just a little up, then lots of down, to Banyuls.

When I passed 500 miles, I stopped to take photos of my GPS. The altitude gain was almost 120,000 feet! Big, black clouds were following me down to the sea, so I didn't want to tarry. I had told my friends that I would turn on my SPOT tracker for my last little bit of the trail. I got into Banyuls and followed the marks to the beach.

I HAD "SPLASH DOWN"! I HAD DONE IT!!!

It was raining, but I didn't care. I sat on the beach and texted and emailed everyone. My friend, Skip, who had given me the inspiring Pyrenees book in the first place, had already sent an email. He said they had watched my "race to the sea" and congratulated me!

I went into a bar along the beach and drank fruit beer. I then checked into a hotel, showered, changed, then treated myself to dinner in a nice restaurant, I'd earned it!!!

Oh yes, there was one more thing I had to do. Contact all my new friends in Barcelona and tell them I was on my way!

For more photos go to: http://still-going-strong.com

2 0 1 4

New Zealand

● ● ●

*"The more I carry the happier I am in camp; the
less I carry the happier I am getting there"*

Sgt. Rock

For more detail on maps, go to: http://still-going-strong.com

March 2014

The Pyke-Big Bay-Hollyford Loop

"This challenging tramping route (88 km) [164 km with the Hollyford loop] is a real adventure for those with a high level of skill and experience. This track is certainly an adventure - please note the following in your trip planning:

This is a challenging tramping route so you will need above average fitness and high level backcountry (remote areas) skills and experience, including navigation and survival skills. You also need river crossing skills and experience.

You need to be well equipped including at least 2 extra days of food in case you are delayed due to weather or flooding. Taking a Personal Locator Beacon and/or mountain radio is essential.

The track is not well defined in places. Some sections flood regularly, making travel impossible for days at a time. Even in good conditions there are several unbridged rivers to cross. Route times are highly variable depending on tramper fitness and ability and weather conditions.

Barrier, Diorite and Pyke Crossing Rivers can be un-crossable even in a medium rain event.

Note that you will encounter knee deep water towards the Alabaster Creek end of the lake during normal lake levels. After rain this becomes very difficult and slow travel. Alabaster Creek is normally crossed via a gravel bar at its mouth. However, after rain this becomes a deep and dangerous crossing. From the head of the lake follow the orange, triangular pole markers through the open areas of flax and tussock until a marked route enters the forest.

The route goes through aptly named 'Black Swamp', then follows an overgrown track up the true left of the Pyke River, through beech forest, flax wetlands and river flats.

The Pyke - Big Bay Route shares a similar natural and social history to the Hollyford Valley. Martins Bay, known to Ngäi Tahu as Kotuku, was an important settlement between 1650 and 1800, with good access to food resources, as well as pounamu (greenstone). Large trees on the river banks were felled to make canoes for use on the lakes. There is ar-chaeological evidence of Maori occupation at Big Bay, including middens and ovens, and some artefacts. It would have been an ideal location for seasonal camps or longer periods of occupation.

The latter half of the 1800s saw exploration of the area by Europeans, with Captain Alabaster, a whaler, being one of the first. In 1886, Martins Bay and Big Bay experienced a small gold rush, with 200 people arriving in the area. However, by the following year only six remained, with the others leaving after poor returns of gold.

Rose bushes and sycamore trees were planted by the early settlers and still survive at Big Bay and Jerusalem Creek.

Department of Conservation Brochure

In 2002, my New Zealand friend, Dianne, and I were hiking west from the Martin's Bay Hut on a track called the Hollyford. It was a sunny day and we were walking along the ocean. We came around a corner and I could see a huge bay in front of us. Dianne told me it was called Big Bay and that there was a hut in the middle of it. Oh, that planted a seed that kept grow-ing for several years!!

The one thing the brochure didn't list about the Pyke Valley was.... sandflies! I think this valley is their favorite breeding ground in all of New Zealand...and that's saying something!

In March of 2014, I put together 10 days of food and drove to Gunn's Camp, at the head of the Hollyford River. All the way out it was rain-ing and cold, and I was a bit concerned even though the forecast was for clearing weather. I met the proprietors and they were excited for me to be doing the Pyke. They said DoC workers had been down a week or so before, so it should be decently marked, and not to worry about the black swamp. Just follow the markers and go straight through it. They also suggested staying along the edges of the lakes and rivers where possible.

For once the weatherman was right. I woke up to a fine blue sky day. It was cold though, and there was fresh snow on the peaks.

My first day was an "easy" one, even though it was 20 kilometers. I left my van at about 10:30am, and hiked down to the Hidden Falls. This part of the trail gets a lot of use and was pretty easy compared to what I was used to. The track went alongside the start of the Hollyford River, with great views across the river at the large, snow-covered Darren Mountains, and glimpses of gorgeous blue water pools in the river. As I crossed Hidden Falls Creek, I could hear the falls but not see them. So I left my pack by the bridge, and hiked a few minutes up the creek. There were the "hidden" falls, with LOTS of water coming down. I sat on a rock near the falls and had my lunch while I enjoyed the view.

The Hidden Falls Hut was about 15 minutes down the track, but I knew I was going to pass that one by and go on to the Alabaster Hut. I followed the track through a section of green mosses and ferns, then through the beech forest until I got to Little Homer Saddle. Then it descended to another waterfall and finally the confluence of the Pyke and Hollyford rivers. There was a fancy (private) hut there, with lots of glass windows and manicured lawns! My not-as-fancy (public) hut was further down the track.

The Alabaster Hut is on the edge of the lake. I had been to this hut several times and knew it would be comfortable and beautiful. Because I was in Fiordland, everywhere I looked was covered with mosses and ferns. A green wonderland. Eileen, a volunteer DoC worker, was at the hut checking passes and doing some cleaning. She had done a great job and the hut was pristine…even the "long drop"!

I left the hut the next morning for day two. My route started out following the edge of Lake Alabaster. After a couple of hours hiking, I thought, "This is a piece of cake!" But I spoke too soon, as the edge of the lake became cliffs and I had to hike up into the bush to get around them. It took me three times as long to do the second half of the lake as the first half. Bush bashing in New Zealand is like going through a jungle. It is slow going, especially if the lay of the land is steep and slippery and next to a lake like this one.

I stopped for a quick lunch when I finally got to the end of the lake. I knew I needed to cross the Alabaster River where it came out of the lake. The description said to cross on the sand bars in the river. When I got to that spot, the wind was blowing across the lake and the river was full of waves and white caps. If there were sand bars there, I sure couldn't see them!

One of the most important things you learn when you are traveling through the backcountry of New Zealand is respect for rivers. They used to call drowning the "settlers' disease" because so many settlers drowned trying to get from one side of a swollen river to the other. It's little wonder I am always very cautious if I have to cross a river.

The river waters weren't flowing very fast, but there were lots of waves coming in from the lake. I figured the sand bars were there, even if I couldn't see them. So I unsnapped my pack's waist belt just in case I had to do some swimming, and using my hiking poles as "feelers" in front of me, I started across. The water was fairly deep, half way up my shorts, but the footing was solid and when the waves came up over my waist I didn't feel unstable. I took it slow and steady all the way across. I was slightly wet and cold afterwards, but at least I had crossed that watery hurdle.

Once I got across the river, lo and behold, there were orange triangles! Yeah! I had something to follow. Sort of. Much of the area was covered with toi toi and flax which was so high, it was over my head. Toi toi is a beautiful tall plant with waving stalks. However the leaves are serrated and can slash your arms and legs. It also had a tendency to trip me by hanging over the track. It was a bit like being a midget in a beautiful maze. If there were markers, they were lost in all this shrubbery. Several times I had to backtrack to find a marker, or to see which way the trail went. No daydreaming allowed down here! And I knew my day wasn't finished yet – I still had "The Black Swamp" to cross before I got to the Olivine Hut.

I stopped for a snack before I crossed the swamp because I figured I might need extra energy. On the web, I had found this wonderfully graphic description of the Black Swamp:

"We'd heard stories about the Black Swamp, and every one of them proved correct. It stank of rotting vegetation; it was, indeed, a very black, swampy area, dotted with odd tussocks of vegetation with strange grassy growths appearing out of the top; and it was waist deep in gooey, quicksand-like mud, as both Rick and I discovered as we waded through it. We started out by trying to hop from clump to clump, but this turned out to be pretty hopeless with the combination of heavy backpack and unstable vegetation, and by the end of the swamp, which can only have been about 200m wide, we were filthy, soaked, and, frankly, having a ball. When you're already muddy, you might as well wallow in it, and wallow in it we did."

Mark Moxon, Long Distance Walks

They were right on! It was gooey, muddy, and deep. You just had to grin and bear it, and slog on through. Once again, I was a little perturbed about how much energy I had spent worrying about this section of the track. Like they said on the web though, by the end of it, I was just laughing! I finally reached the Olivine Hut at 7:30pm – a long but successful day.

I had a bit of a sleep in on Day Three, and didn't leave the hut until 10:00am. That's late for me! My first obstacle was the "flying fox". A flying fox is a way to cross a big river: You climb way up in a tree where there is a small metal "car" for you and your pack. You sit in this buggy while you turn a crank that moves it (with you in it) across the river on a cable. It was fun to cross the river high in the air!

I had another lake to get around that day; Lake Wilmot. There were lots of ups and downs to get to the other side, so it seemed to take forever. I found a rock bivy up on the side of the lake, but I was there early enough and the weather was still so clear that I decided to go further and camp alongside the Pyke River.

My back was bothering me. It sometimes went into spasm thanks to a couple of twisted ribs, so I was having a hard time "seeing straight"! When my back does this, I know I will have to endure 24 to 48 hours of bother. I have several remedies, including a back magnet, a battery operated mini-masseuse, and a couple of hand balls to roll on. But I know I just have to endure the pain till it gets better...which it usually does after a couple of days.

I pressed on, but in hindsight, I would have been better off to stay at the rock shelter. It was hard to find a level spot to pitch my tent, but I finally found a decent place alongside the river. It had been clear and there wasn't anything on the horizon, so I didn't think the water would come up during the night. Just in case, I put a stick in the sand at the water's edge.

That way I could shine my flashlight on the stick and see if the water level had changed.

I thought it was a decent campsite until the sandflies found me! They were hungry, and I was the only red meat around. I slathered myself with my homemade bug repellant, then fixed a hurried dinner. As I dove into my tent, I found about 200 sandflies had sneaked in the open door. Reminder to self, Talie – shut the tent door in sandfly zones! It took 30 minutes of squashing sandflies before I could relax.

The next morning, I awoke early so I could be up before the sandflies. I wasn't early enough. While I was packing up my tent, I discovered about 30 sandflies doing the backstroke in my cup of tea! Bummer! Once I got moving, they didn't bother me as much.

The hiking for this day wasn't steep, but it was difficult once I factored in that I had to keep one eye out for track markers, and one eye on the trail. The ferns were hiding rocks, logs and holes. I often fell down because I couldn't see my feet as I tripped or stepped into a hole. I also had several river crossings – some mid-thigh deep. But the rivers were not flowing fast and it was simply a case of walking through the water. Because it hadn't rained for the last couple of days, the water was crystal clear, and I could see every rock a meter deep in the river.

I had to cross Pyke River, and was nervous it might be bigger than the side streams I had crossed. It was further across and the water was flowing fairly fast, but it didn't look more than knee level deep. No problem! But as I was crossing, I slipped on a rock and fell down. I wasn't swept away or anything, but the water was going over my back. I tried to get up, but slipped again. I eventually managed to get vertical and work my way across, relieved there had been no one there to laugh at me! But now, I was soaked along with my pack. Luckily I was wearing my waterproof Aarn pack, so all my gear was protected inside.

From that point, I had a track to follow downhill to Big Bay. It was a real luxury to actually be on a marked track. Along the way, I met a hunter who was looking for deer. He asked if I had seen any, but I had probably been making so much noise that any deer would have shied away from me! He told me it was getting near high tide and that I should probably take the 25 minute detour to the three-wire bridge in order to get to the hut. He also invited me over to his hut the next day for a cup of tea. Such a Kiwi thing to do!

When I got to the bay following the river, I looked at the water level. It was calm, and even though it wasn't crystal clear like the streams I had crossed, it still looked doable. With my trusty poles out in front of me, I worked my way across the mouth of the river. It didn't get as deep as some of the rivers I had crossed, and I was glad I could save myself a 25 minute walk to the three-wire bridge.

From that last river crossing, things started getting really confusing. There were multiple "roads" going every which way, and lots of private huts. I didn't realize so many people flew or boated in. Even though it had taken me four solid days of tramping to get here, I was definitely not isolated! I wandered around, checking my GPS, to find the DoC hut, and finally, at 6:00pm, there it was...the hut I had been dreaming about since that day in 2002 when Dianne and I were over at Martin's Bay. It wasn't one of the newer huts, and it was a bit tired, but it was the BIG BAY HUT!

Three hunters were staying there. They had flown in, and were amazed I had walked all the way. My tights, which I had been wearing under my shorts, were shredded from the toi toi and flax, so I looked pretty funny.

The next day was a rest day for me at Big Bay. I didn't work hard to get here just to leave right away! And believe it or not, this was the only day on this trip that it rained a little bit. I hung out my tent to dry in between rain showers, and then went out to the beach to see the bay. It was huge! I could look back up the Pyke Valley and see the mountains where I had started my trip. But my real excitement was to be looking at Big Bay, knowing I had survived the Pyke Valley to get here!

From the beach, I wandered over to the private hut where Graham the hunter, and his friends, were staying. Wow, there was a big difference between the DoC hut and the private huts. They had a generator for electricity, refrigerator, and a stove! I even enjoyed a couple of cold beers with them. When they told me they were flying home to Christchurch the next day in a private plane, I asked if they could possibly take my tent. I wouldn't be needing it for the rest of the hike and it would be great to not have to carry it. I told them I could pick it up after I got out, but Graham said he'd drop it off at my friends' house in Christchurch. What service! I love these Kiwis!!

On Day Six, I packed up my gear again (without my tent!) and headed around the bay. I knew I should be able to follow the beach all the way to the Hollyford Track and Martins Bay Hut. My track description said there were a couple of river crossings along the bay that could be high after rain. I was a little worried about them, but they were not high and a real non-issue. I loved the level beach walking, even on the spots where I had to go over small boulders.

About 10:00am, the clouds cleared off and it was BEAUTIFUL! I kept thinking this was one of the best days of my whole life. I was walking around Big Bay in Fiordland, I had completed the hardest part of this trip in the Pyke Valley, and the rest was going to be fun. I was practically skipping! When I stopped for lunch, I took off my boots, found a little rock pool and soaked my feet. It was fun seeing little ocean critters in the pools. I knew I had all day to get to the hut, and I planned on enjoying my beach walk along the way. I met three young German trampers who were doing the Pyke from the other direction. I shared my experiences with them and told them to "enjoy the black swamp"!

Before I got to Martins Bay, there was a rocky point to navigate around. A seal colony lived in the rocks. You can usually smell and hear a seal colony long before you see them. When Dianne and I were here 11 years ago, we saw some yellow-crested penguins as well. So, when I got close to the rocks, I slowed down and tried to be a bit quieter. Shhh. No more shouting for joy on this greatest day!! Sure enough, there was a cute little penguin hiding in the rocks. I watched him, and he watched me, for about 15 minutes. Magic.

Then I went on and saw the seal colony. There were lots of cute little pups swimming in the pools and climbing on the rocks. The mom seals were sunning themselves and not paying a bit of attention to me or the pups! But, being respectful of wildlife, I kept my distance so as not to frighten them.

Just past the seal colony, a sign marked the end of the Pyke Trail. It was fun to read the other side that listed the warnings about the tramp. It made me feel really happy to have survived it!

Just before the hut, I met a guided group, mostly from America. I told the guide where I had seen the penguin and he hoped they would see it too. Their main aim, however, was to see the seal colony. The group had come in by boat and were flying out later that evening. They were definitely a lot cleaner, and smelled better, than me!

When I got to the Martins Bay Hut, I was surprised at all the people there. Most had flown in (there is a small airstrip nearby), or had taken jet boats down the Hollyford River and across Lake McKerrow. Some had hiked down but were taking planes out, while others had taken planes in and were hiking out. It was fun meeting so many trampers. I had planned an extra day at Martins Bay, so I had a very relaxing day in a beautiful spot.

The hut was right above a small spit which protected the area from the ocean waves; I had read it was not advisable to swim in the ocean right there because of the currents. I walked up the beach until the water was calm and had a lovely day splashing about and sitting in the sun. It was so good to look across the water, through the flax, to see snow-capped mountains. Definitely "sea to summit"!

My next two days followed an aptly named track: The Demon Track. When Dianne and I were here in 2002, we had flown down and then taken the jet boat across Lake McKerrow, so I had missed this part of the Hollyford. With a name like that, it certainly struck my fancy. I wonder why? DoC brochures describe the Demon Trail as:

> ... *A historical cattle track. This section is both rocky and undulating but there are long sections of formed, flat track in-between. It can be difficult underfoot in wet weather, with the track becoming slippery and with loose rocks. Some of the creek crossings can be dangerous, so extreme care is required - using the three-wire bridges is recommended. After heavy rain some creeks may be impassable.*

I'm on it!!

From the Martins Bay Hut, I followed the track around Lake McKerrow. I had a couple of creek crossings ahead of me, but there were plenty of three-wire bridges, and I was starting to look forward to them. The lake shore passed the place where the old settlement of Jamestown was. Another three-wire crossing, and I was at the Hokuri Hut.

There were two groups of trampers going the same way as me that day, one with 10 people and the other with five. That's a lot of people using a hut each night, so I thought if I could skip a hut I would put myself a day ahead of them. Thus, I stopped for lunch at the Hokuri Hut and continued on to the Demon Trail Hut. They were right about this section being difficult underfoot, and I was glad it wasn't raining. I had multiple three-wire bridges to cross, but I got to the Demon Trail Hut at 7:00pm, after an 11 hour day. There were only four other people at the hut, so pushing on had been a good choice…apart from the fact that two of my hut mates snored!

The next day, Day Nine, was a leisurely hike and I got to the Alabaster Hut at 5:00pm. I met up with the German trampers I had passed going from Martins Bay to Big Bay. We shared stories about the Pyke and the Black Swamp. They were stunned I had done it solo at age 67!

Since I still had one more day of food, I decided to stop at the Hidden Falls Hut on the way out. It was another full hut – 15 people with bunk space for 12, meaning three people were "camped out" on the floor. It rained hard and everyone was glad to be indoors where it was dry. I could hardly believe that I had done almost the full Pyke - Big Bay Loop without a single day of walking in the rain! I had enjoyed 10 blue sky days, almost unheard of in Fiordland. So, on the final morning, it wasn't too hard to don my rain gear and slog the last two hours back to my van. I stopped at Gunn's Camp to let them know I had successfully completed the loop. I was a happy tramper!

For more photos go to: http://still-going-strong.com

New Zealand

● ● ●

Yes, the race is long – to finish first, first you must finish.

The Art of Racing in the Rain

In 2002, I first hiked the new Hump Ridge Track in the very south of the South Island. I had climbed up to the Okara Hut and spent the first night there. The next morning was unusually clear, and I was able to go to the top of the "Hump" and see spectacular views, all the way to Stewart Island. Looking in the other direction, I noticed a beautiful lake surrounded by bush (that's Kiwi for forest). "Where is that?" I thought. "I want to go there!" I asked the people at the hut and found out it was named Lake Poteriteri. I knew it was a place I had to explore in the future. View from the Hump Ridge:

January 2015

Lake Poteriteri

So now we fast forward to 2015, and I had put together a trip to Lake Poteriteri. I talked with my friends, Johan and Joyce, and arranged for Wairarahiri Jet Boats to take me across Lake Hauroko and down part of the Wairarahiri River. There, Johan would drop me off and I could hike over land to Lake Poteriteri. I had plans to go from the hut on Lake Poteriteri to a hut on the Slaughterburn River; a full day of bush bashing because there was no trail. Then I would hike down to the Waitutu Hut, out to Westies Hut, back to Waitutu, and then to the Wairarahiri Hut. Johan would then pick me up and bring me back up the river to my vehicle. I planned a full 10 days in the bush, so once again, my pack was heavy!

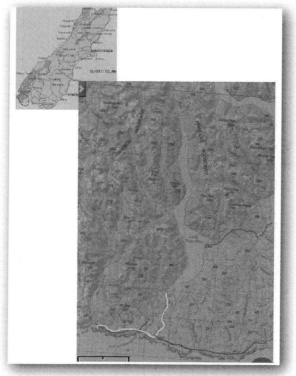

For more detail on maps, go to: http://still-going-strong.com

Johan let me park my van at his house and we drove up to Lake Hauroko from there. He had an almost full load for his jet boat tour that day. He takes people all the way down the Wairarahiri River for lunch and back. It's a very popular trip so I was lucky to be able to squeeze in with them for part of the trip.

We started down the Wairarahiri River, and Johan said he would drop me closest to the track going to Poteriteri. This was further down the river, past the three-wire bridge on the track. Johan maneuvered the jet boat along the bank, and I hopped off. I tried to get my pack from the boat, but it was too heavy to pull up the slippery side. One of the men on board helped me hoist it on to the bank. I saw some shocked expressions as the jet boat took off again. They were astounded I was going into that dense wilderness by myself!

I did a fair amount of bush bashing until I found the track to Lake Poteriteri. It was very rough, as not many people got out there, but I was able to follow it fairly well. When a track isn't used a lot, the ferns become overgrown. I couldn't see the ground because of the ferns, thus I kept tripping on logs or stepping into holes. This forced me to slow down and be extra cautious.

I got to the Lake Poteriteri Hut at about 8:00pm. A DoC ranger named Steve was staying there, working on the trail and doing pest control counts. His eyes got really big when I walked in that evening. He had come in by helicopter, and as this was a really remote hut, he didn't expect anyone, especially a 68 year old female American solo trekker!

Steve immediately started clearing off one of the bunks, but I told him that wasn't necessary. I would hang my hammock out in the trees and only come into the hut to fix meals, and hide out from the sandflies and mosquitos. There were plenty of perfect hammock spots right along the lake edge, so I could sleep and look out to see the lake when I woke up. I was ecstatic. I had FINALLY made it to Lake Poteriteri!

After setting up my hammock, I went back into the hut. When I read the entries in the hut book, I discovered it would probably take two days to get to the Slaughterburn Hut. The reports also said it was pretty rough going. It looked like I had my work cut out for me. Many of the trampers said to be sure you had a compass. Once again…WHAT was I letting myself in for?

The next day, while Steve went out to clear some of the overgrown track, I took hikes along the lake's edge. There were plenty of geese, and they'd left obvious signs on the beach where they had been hanging out - lots of poop! Since the lake was the water source for cooking and drinking, I got my water by wading out into the lake, well past the geese poop.

I spent a couple of hours going along the edge of Lake Poteriteri, crossing some inlet streams and taking in the views. I could see the Princess Mountains to the northeast, and the Cameron Mountains to the northwest. I was surrounded by mountains, including the ridge I would hike over to get to Slaughterburn.

Steve was a typically friendly and generous Kiwi bloke. We had fun comparing trips we had done in the South Island. Because he had come in by helicopter, he had a cooler full of fresh food. He fixed chicken (real chicken - not dehydrated!) and noodles for dinner, and he made enough to share with me. What a treat to have fresh food when tramping! I was very appreciative!

While we were talking, Steve mentioned a helicopter was coming in the next day to take him and another ranger to the Grant Burn. When I checked on the map, I discovered it was near the South Coast Track. He said I might be able to hitch a ride if there was room. Oh, a helicopter from Heaven!!! I was sure hoping there would be room! I was not looking forward to two days of bush bashing to get to the Slaughterburn Hut.

I was already packed and ready to go when the helicopter landed the next morning. I timidly asked the pilot if I could hitch a ride, and when he said, "Sure, hop in." I could have jumped for joy! I didn't want to make waves, so I told the pilot to drop me where he dropped Steve and the other DoC worker. I could figure out my way to the track from there. It was great fun looking down on the rest of Lake Poteriteri and the "rough going" ridge that I would have been working my way along.

Since the Grant Burn drop off spot was so close to the South Coast Track, I decided to change my plan. Instead of going to Slaughterburn right away, I chose to go to Westies Hut from the Grant Burn. I'd pick up the Slaughterburn on my way back.

There was a bit of bush bashing to get from where the helicopter dropped us off. It was in the middle of nowhere! I had my GPS on, so I could see what direction to go to get to the South Coast Track. I wandered among the ferns, scrub, and small trees, until finally, I saw an orange triangle. I could have kissed that little piece of plastic! I figured I had about six kilometers along the track to get to Westies Hut.

The South Coast Track is beautiful. Because it is along the southern coast, it is very lush and green, with lots of ferns, podocarps, and mosses. Are you getting tired of me describing the tracks like this? I guess it's because that's the way they are! The track didn't go along the seashore, which is rocky and bluffed. It was inland enough that most of the time I couldn't actually see the ocean, but occasionally there was a glimpse of the seashore.

Westies Hut is another little gem in the New Zealand backcountry. I had seen a video of Westies on the New Zealand news one night. They talked about its remoteness, and that it was the most southern AND most western hut on the South Island. That really increased my desire to get there!

According to my map, Westies was on the east side of Prices Harbor. But when I got to that point, there was no hut! Before I left on this adventure, I had taken photos of the descriptions in Moir's Guide South. So, I looked at those, and read: "Westies Hut, a four bunk hut built in a cave a little above the high tide mark, can be found at the west end of Prices Harbor, opposite the island a little offshore." Thus my map program showed Westies in the wrong spot. Good thing I had a copy of the book!

I continued on, till I found a lovely marker with "Westies" written on it. There was a separate little track off the South Coast Track leading down to the hut. It took about 15 minutes on this side track to lead me to the edge of the coast. There was quite a drop off to hike down to the ocean, and as I got closer and closer I became more nervous. But when I reached the cliffs, I found ropes to hold onto in the steepest parts. My friends will tell you that I am not usually happy about clinging onto ropes along a steep bank, but I was loving these ones! I was even happier when I got all the way down to the beach level.

What a cool little hut in a unique spot! It was well worth the trip to get there. Westies is actually built in a bit of a cave right above the high tide line. It is a not a DoC hut, so it is privately maintained. Whenever I am in a hut, whether it is DoC or not, I do my best to make it tidier and better than when I got there. So my first order of business at Westies was to tidy up a bit.

The notes in the hut talked about turning on the water system. Upon further investigation, I saw all the hoses and connections to run water into a sink inside the hut. After opening up everything, the water should have been running. Alas, it was not. So I followed the hoses to the intake, which was a tank on the hill. The tank wasn't full, so I followed the next set of hoses to the intake for the tank. Because it was the end of the summer, there was not enough water coming out of the spring to fill the tank. Oh, well....

I took a hike along the beach to where it looked like water was coming down from the cliffs. Sure enough, there was lots of water in that little stream. I filled all the available bottles and containers and took them back to Westies. At least I would have enough water to cook, drink and clean with. As for cleaning my muddy body, there was plenty of ocean water!

Westies had a wood burning stove, so I gathered enough wood to make a small fire - just enough to take the chill off. After eating my supper, I took my cup of tea to the beach to watch the sun go down, and to see the waves crash on the rocky shore. I had a lovely evening all alone in the hut that night. The waves on the beach created a wonderful "white noise", which lulled me to sleep.

The next day, I packed a day pack and hiked up the trail to the top of the cliffs. I followed the South Coast Track to where it ends on the maps: Big River. I think there is a track that actually goes up the river, but I stopped before crossing. My original goal had been to see Big River, and I felt I had achieved that. Then I came back and watched seals and oyster catchers play in the surf. Oyster catchers are cute little sea birds with red beaks, but they can be very noisy if you disturb their nests, as I discovered one time on Stewart Island!

That second night at Westies, some other hikers, Diane, Hans and Sami, joined me. Johan had dropped them at the South Coast Track the day after me and they'd hiked straight out to Westies. They had dropped a food bag at the Waitutu Hut for their hike back and were hoping no one would take it. Hans also investigated the water system. He came to the same conclusion I had: not enough water in the spring. Sami spent a good deal of time gathering wood so she could warm up, and we had a very cozy night in the hut.

On Day Five, I left at 8:45am in light, misty rain. Going through the scrub had me soaked even before the climb to the top of the cliffs. Luckily the ropes weren't wet and I could still get up the steep trail. It rained most of the day so it was a real slog. I kept trying to remind myself that the beauty of the South Coast is due to its wet environment. But most of the time, I just put my head down and watched the water pour off my rain hood. When I finally got to Waitutu Hut, the sun came out and I could hang out my wet clothes on the porch. Sure enough, there was Hans' extra food bag. I thought that was such a great idea, I decided to do the same thing.

Since I had missed the Slaughterburn Hut because of my helicopter ride, I wanted to hike up there. There wasn't an official route, but the comments in the hut book had said to "follow a trapper's line". I took photos of the description in the hut book so I could refer to it while hiking.

Some of New Zealand's biggest pests are possums, stoats and rats, introduced when man arrived on the islands. Since then, they have become huge threats to New Zealand's natural environment. Possums, rats and stoats have no predators in New Zealand, and lots of very palatable vegetation and ground nesting birds to devour. One of the methods of controlling these pests is to put out traps and I was going to follow one of these trapper's lines.

A trapper's line is not exactly a trail. Rather, it's a route through the bush, marked with yellow plastic triangles, as opposed to orange triangles on a DoC track. According to the hut book, the line followed the Waitutu River up to the Slaughterburn River. I also knew from my description in the Moir's Guide, that I should follow the river. I had never followed a trappers' line, so this was all new to me! And since it wasn't a track or trail, it was pretty wild. I activated the recording part of my GPS maps. That way, if I got "misplaced" (a wonderful alternative to "lost"), I could check my map and find my way back. I love being able to use a GPS! The trapper's line was fairly well marked and only a couple of times did I need to search for the next marker.

The trapper's line joined a DoC track shortly before the Slaughterburn confluence. There was actually a three-wire bridge across the Waitutu with something I had never seen before: a "possum stop gate"! Possums can cross three-wire bridges too?? Really? I found it hard to believe, but the gate really was there. Of course I had to cross the three-wire just to check out the gate and see how it worked. Sure enough, you can balance on a three wire and open and shut a gate!

Even though the track had been a little rough, I got to the hut about 2:30 in the afternoon. It had been a beautiful day, much better than my slog the day before. According to the Slaughterburn Hut book, the last person had been there six weeks before. Obviously not a very well used hut! And, as I looked through the entries since 2009, I discovered I was the first person from the USA. In all of 2014, there had been only 36 people there for a total of 57 nights (including eight DoC Workers for 21 nights.) It didn't get much more remote than this, and I decided I had finally gotten "out there". Of course, I was ecstatic!

The next day, I explored the area. I went back down to the Waitutu and crossed on the three-wire bridge, laughing about the possum stop gate as I went! I followed the track for a while, but according to my information, it only went a little way up the river. I didn't want to do much bush bashing in that remote part of Fiordland. I had been pretty lucky not to get lost so far, and I didn't want to push my luck. So I went back to the hut and enjoyed a relaxing day in the sunshine.

Did I say "Relaxing day in the sunshine"?? Yeah, right! One of the other residents of Fiordland is the sandfly. So in order to relax in the sunshine, I had to coat myself with bug repellent first. It wasn't that effective, and before long, I was relaxing inside the Slaughterburn Hut!

After two days at this lovely hut, it was pretty hard to leave. I now think it is one of my favorite huts (let's see – how many times have I said that about other huts?) I headed out under blue skies and stopped for lunch by the Waitutu River. The clouds moved in while I was eating, and it started to rain. And then, a few minutes after taking off, I lost the track on the trapper's line. I wandered to and fro, going back to the last marker three times and looking for the next one. Finally, I opened up the GPS on my phone and was able to locate the track. This would not be a good place to get lost! After that, I made a point of keeping my eye on the yellow markers.

It rained pretty hard at the Waitutu Hut that night, and the next day, Day 9, the rains totally set in. There is a lovely anonymous New Zealand poem which I read for the first time in the Okaka Hut, on the Hump Ridge Track. I have since seen this poem in several places - it perfectly describes a rainy day in Fiordland:

It rained and rained and rained and rained
The average fall was well maintained
And when the tracks were simply bogs
It started raining cats and dogs

After a drought of half an hour
We had a most refreshing shower
And then, the most curious thing of all
A gentle rain began to fall

Next day was also fairly dry
Save for a deluge from the sky
Which wetted the party to the skin
And after that the rain set in!

For me, it was another long, wet slog to get to the Wairarahiri Hut. This was to be the last stop on my trip, and I was glad I had allowed an extra day to get here. On these trips, I plan extra days for two main reasons. First, if I should get stuck and unable to cross a swollen river, it is good to have time built into the trip itinerary. Second, if I don't need the extra day, I can always enjoy a day off at a beautiful place like Poteriteri, Westies, or Slaughterburn.

Fortunately, the next day was sunny, so I washed my soggy clothes and hung them out to dry. I also washed my hair, gathered firewood, and cleaned the wood shed. I even walked to the beach for lunch and gathered more firewood along the way. In the afternoon, I walked down to the private Waitutu Lodge and enjoyed a chat with the caretakers, Peter and Rose, and Tiara their granddaughter. That evening, I finished off my last dinner from my food bag, and was proud of myself for planning my meals perfectly.

On Day 11, I hiked down a short way (1.5 kilometers) to join Johan and his new group of clients for lunch at the Waitutu Lodge. He cooked a delicious meal, and after 10 days of dehydrated food, I totally enjoyed the "freshies!" Then I was happy to ride in the jet boat and go back to where I had left my van so many days before.

For more photos go to: http://still-going-strong.com

Earthquake Zones

● ● ●

The difference between what we do and what we are capable of doing
Would suffice to solve most of the world's problems.

Mohandas Gandhi

AFTER BEING TOO CLOSE FOR comfort to four big earthquakes, some of my friends now say they don't want to travel with me. I wonder why? But I tell them, "I am a survivor. So I am the person you really want to be with in an earthquake!"

The first big earthquake I experienced occurred in Maui, Hawaii in October of 2006. My class of 1964 was having a celebration, because 2006 was the year we turned 60. I was staying with one of my classmates, Sylvia, who had a home on Maui. At 7:00am, I was in the process of getting up and making my bed. The vertical blinds started shaking and I thought the wind was blowing. When things started falling off the shelves, I realized it was an earthquake. I yelled to Sylvia, "GET OUT! It's an earthquake!" and ran out the front door. I had never seen cars bounce on their wheels before. It was a very strange phenomenon for me, but Sylvia wasn't too concerned. She didn't even get out of bed! Luckily, there was no structural damage to the house, but I was freaked out. The electricity was off and none of the traffic lights were working, so it was hard to get across the island to where my classmates were staying. For all the drama, everything on Maui was pretty much back to normal by the end of the day.

On February 27, 2010, I was backpacking outside of El Bolson, Argentina. The next day, when I got in a taxi at the trail's end to go back to El Bolson, the taxi driver kept saying:

"Terremoto, terremoto. Ocho punto ocho!"

Even though my Spanish was limited, I still knew what he was saying:

"Earthquake, earthquake. 8.8!"

It was the fifth largest earthquake ever recorded on a seismograph. By the time I was able to get onto the internet, my kids and friends had all sent messages to find out if I was ok. But, to tell the truth, I never even felt it.

Later that year, on September 4, I was in Christchurch, New Zealand. I was sound asleep at my friends', Myles and Margaret's, home. I awoke abruptly, feeling like I was in a washing machine – an incredibly noisy washing machine! At that point, my understanding of what you should do in an earthquake was to stand in a doorway. There was no way I could get to the doorway. Things were shaking so bad I couldn't get out of bed, much less stand up. It seemed to last a really long time, but I found out later it was less than a minute. In a situation like that, a minute is a long time! The earthquake showed 7.1 on the seismograph. When it stopped, I called to Myles and Margaret, whose bedroom was across the hall, "Are you ok?" Their answer was, "Yes, how about you?" We were all pretty freaked out and it was still very dark.

There was no electricity. We'd have to wait till it was light to see what kind of damage there was. Myles had a battery operated radio, so we could hear news of what was happening. I went into their bedroom and actually got in bed with them. Luckily our cell phones were still working. While they called their kids, I sent text messages to Craig and Steve. I got a text right back saying they had heard about the earthquake, and were glad I was ok. I am amazed how quickly news travels around the globe in this day and age!

Even before it was light, there was a knock on the door. It was a neighbor, checking to make sure we were all right. We were fine. Thankfully, they were ok too.

Myles and Margaret's home was over 100 years old, but since it was a wood frame house, there was only minor damage. The top of the brick chimney fell, but they were REALLY lucky that it fell away from the house rather than into the living room. Myles had attached cables to their TV, so it was stabilized. Things had fallen off shelves and a couple of items had shattered, but considering we were only a few miles from the epicenter, we were pretty lucky.

This earthquake did a lot of damage around Christchurch. Over the next couple of days, we witnessed scenes of terrible destruction around the city. But, almost miraculously, there had been no loss of life. Because of the time the earthquake occurred – 5:00am – most people were asleep in their homes, and not at work, in school, or on the streets. If it had happened later in the day, dozens of lives would have been lost.

Christchurch had many beautiful stone buildings, some of which had been there for a hundred years or more – old by New Zealand standards. Most of them were damaged. The magnificent Cathedral in the center of the city had been very hard hit. Myles and Margaret's church had been of brick construction and was totally destroyed.

For months after that first earthquake, there were aftershocks, some of which were pretty unsettling. With all the information that came out in the aftermath, I probably learned more than I wanted to know about earthquakes. For example, I have learned there is what they call the "triangle of safety" if you are in an earthquake. If you can't get outside, the biggest worry is having the ceiling or roof come down on top of you. So, if you lie on the ground right up against a couch, bed, or other solid piece of furniture, there is a good possibility there will be a "triangle" of space next to the furniture that you can survive in.

That trip to New Zealand ended in February, 2011 when I flew back to the USA. Several days after I left, Christchurch suffered another big earthquake on February 22. It happened in the middle of the day, and 185 people were killed. To this day, the middle of Christchurch resembles a gigantic construction site as they slowly rebuild this beautiful city. In the meantime, many city retailers have set up temporary shops in shipping containers. Kiwis sure are resourceful!

NEPAL

APRIL – MAY 2015

In the spring of 2015, I had put together a trip to India and Nepal. On April 25, my friend, Ishor, and I were on a bus between Kathmandu and Kamari. I was going to visit the village of Tintale where I had been instrumental in starting a school and having clean air cook-stoves installed.

We stopped for a lunch break at a roadside restaurant. We had ordered dal bhat, the local fast food consisting of lentils (dal) and steamed rice (bhat), and were waiting for our order. I thought Ishor was shaking the table, and he thought I was the culprit. At the same time, when we realized the shaking was caused by other forces, we looked at each other and shouted.

"EARTHQUAKE!"

Everyone sprinted outside. The bus was bouncing on its wheels. Trees and power poles were swaying back and forth. I could feel the ground moving under my feet. There was no structural damage, so we went back into the restaurant. We knew it had been a big 'quake, but we didn't know where the epicenter was, or how much damage there might be in other places. After we had finished our lunch, we continued our bus journey to Tintale village.

Even in the remote villages of Nepal, there was immediate communication, and I was able to contact my kids and friends and tell them I was ok. When we got to Katari, we switched on the television in our guest-house and saw the devastation in Kathmandu. Earlier that morning, at 5:00am, Ishor and I had walked across Patan Square in Kathmandu to get to our bus. Seven hours later, at 12 noon, they estimated 900 people had been killed in Patan Square when the earthquake hit. That was a little too close for comfort for me.

Ishor and I had planned to return to Kathmandu after five days in Tintale Village. I had seen the news reports, and Ishor had talked to his family. He felt we would be safe, but I was quite nervous. Anything could happen if we returned to a disaster zone. I had left some luggage at my hotel in Patan Square, so I wondered if I would be able to locate my gear. But my biggest concern was whether we would have water and food. So, when we stopped in Katari, I bought extra bottles of water and some noodles. Coming back into Kathmandu on the bus, we could see devastation, but I was able to get to my hotel.

While I was in Tintale, I had an idea that if I could get my friends to pledge money to me, I could help with earthquake relief. If the ATMs still worked in Kathmandu, I would be able to withdraw cash to spend, knowing that when I got home, I could collect the pledges from my friends to replenish my accounts. I went on Facebook and posted that if anyone wanted to pledge money to me, I would make sure that 100% of it would go to the Nepalese people as earthquake relief.

Social media sure works fast. Before we got back to Kathmandu I had several thousand dollars in pledges from the USA, Germany, England, and New Zealand. Then, when Ishor and I were touring the little village of Sakhu, which had been totally destroyed, a lady came up to me and asked about what I was doing. Then she asked if she could interview me. She was with the BBC! That really helped my pledges!

The first relief I funded was food for the people in Sakhu. These people were barely scraping by even before the earthquake. Then, after the earthquake, some had lost family members, their homes, and now their jobs. They really had nothing.

Ishor and I met with one of the locals in Sakhu. He identified the families most in need, and helped us put together a list of what to buy. I think that while we were in Sakhu, among the devastation, was when we were most at risk. We had to go down some alleyways that were covered with rubble and the buildings above us were totally unstable. I ducked my head, said a prayer, and followed on...

Then onto the back of Ishor's motorbike for the ride into Kathmandu, (maybe that was even more dangerous!), and to the ATMs for more cash. Disaster relief was a new one for me, and I made it up as I went. One of the big things I learned was that by being on the ground, I was helping in two ways: by purchasing relief items from the locals, I was putting money back into the hands of the people. I was also getting food and supplies directly to those most in need. The only things we could not find in all of Kathmandu were tarpaulins and water purification tablets, and we looked everywhere!

Even though it was a sad time, it was a very rewarding experience for me. One of the key factors was having locals to work with; they knew what was needed and where it was needed. Our contacts in Sakhu asked us to bring in supplies under cover of darkness, so that people who already had food wouldn't line up to get ours. Ishor and I looked all over Kathmandu for a truck driver who would deliver after dark, but, alas, no one would go at night. When we called Sakhu and told them, they said they could get a vehicle to come and get most of the food. They came in a bus!

Now, Kathmandu, like most developing big cities, has very narrow streets. I wish you could have seen that bus navigating through the little alleyways. They even had one young man sitting on top of the bus to be sure the hanging wires didn't get hooked on the top. I called it "The Rice Bus"!

The following day, Ishor and I again rode through Kathmandu and located the rest of the items on our relief list: water, soap, and medicines. We were able to hire a truck to drive those items to Sakhu, as it was during daylight hours. Once there, we helped distribute the food and supplies to those who needed it

By this time, I had raised about $4,500, and pledges were still coming in. I joined my Sherpa friend, Pemba, to do some trekking around the Annapurna Circuit, and watched the sunrise on Dhaulagiri. That trek ended in the lakeside town of Pokhara, where I was able to source the tarps and water purification I had not been able to find in Kathmandu.

After more distribution of relief supplies, I started the trek that had instigated this whole trip. My Sherpa friend from Crested Butte was taking a group of us to Tengboche Monastery to see Mt. Everest.

While trekking from Lukla to Tengboche Monastery, I was able to physically help the locals. The trekking group helped remove furniture, doors, and windows from a building that needed to be demolished. We then delivered tarps to a remote village across the river from Ghat. A couple of days later we returned to Ghat, and worked with the locals to cut a new trail through a landslide caused by the earthquake. My pledges helped to pay the local men for a hard day's work, and again, it was good to get money directly into their hands.

The final portion of my relief efforts was to arrange for 60 bags of cement to be delivered to that remote village past Ghat. A bag of cement costing $6 in Kathmandu would cost $75 by the time you transported it to the building site: first to the airport, then fly it to Lukla, then porters to carry it to Ghat, and then more porters to get it across the river. Nothing is easy in that part of the world!

I sure hope my earthquake experiences are complete. But I have learned that when the universe wants to put me where I can be of help, I had better be ready to roll up my sleeves.

For more photos go to: http://still-going-strong.com

United States

● ● ●

TWENTY YEARS FROM NOW
YOU WILL BE MORE DISAPPOINTED
BY THE THINGS YOU DIDN'T DO
THAN BY THE ONES YOU DID.

SO THROW OFF THE BOW LINES.
SAIL AWAY FROM THE SAFE HARBOR.
CATCH THE TRADE WINDS IN YOUR SAILS.

EXPLORE. DREAM.
DISCOVER.

Mark Twain

July – August 2015

The Colorado Trail

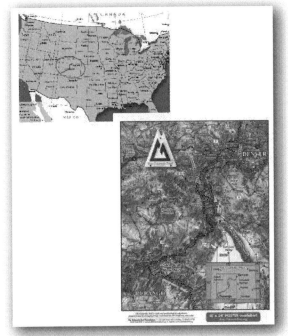

For more detail on maps, go to: http://still-going-strong.com

The Colorado Trail is Colorado's premier long distance trail. Stretching almost 500 miles from Denver to Durango, it travels through the spectacular Colorado Rocky Mountains amongst peaks with lakes, creeks and diverse ecosystems. Trail users experience six wilderness areas and eight mountain ranges topping out at 13,271 feet, just below Coney Summit at 13,334 feet. The average elevation is over 10,000 feet and it rises and falls dramatically. Users traveling from Denver to Durango will climb 89,354 feet.

Colorado Trail Foundation

Three years after doing the Haute Route through the Pyrenees, I was itching to do another long trail. I had no desire to do the Appalachian Trail, or the Continental Divide Trail, or the Pacific Crest Trail. However, I did like the look of the Colorado Trail. It was closer to home…in my own home state, to be exact! So, why not hike across Colorado? There were mountains, streams, forests, wildflowers, and wild animals. What else could I possibly want?

I knew the Colorado Trail would be a lot different from the Haute Route. This time round, there'd be no staffed huts. That meant no big dinners, no occasional showers, no breakfast with coffee, no sandwiches for lunch along the way. All my food would have to be carried by me. I had carried a tent on the Haute Route, so at least that part wasn't any different.

Hiking At Home
Originally, I gave myself 60 days to hike from Denver to Durango. The length of the trail was 485 miles, a little less than the 500 miles I had done in the Pyrenees. Since it had taken me 55 days to hike the Haute Route, 60 days seemed like a manageable time span.

Of course, not every plan goes without a hitch. With one call from my son, Craig, I lost the first week: "Hey Mom, I'm doing a workshop in Denver. Why don't you come and assist?" Well, any of you moms out there know that when our grown children ask us for something like that, the answer is always, "Yes. Of course." So instead of starting the trail on July 6, it was backed up to July 13. Not a problem…

Then I had a call from my son, Steve, who said, "Hey, Mom, Gates is getting his black belt in karate on August 29. We would love you to come for the ceremony!" And the answer was, "Yes. Of course." And that was how I lost the last week of the trail, turning 60 days into 42 days.

485 miles over 42 days meant that I would have to average 11.5 miles a day. With a heavy pack and going over altitude (the trail has 89,345 feet of elevation gain – again not quite as much as the Pyrenees), I thought I might struggle to get 11.5 miles per day. But on days of more flat or down-hill hiking, 11.5 miles would be totally doable. So we were still on track. Excuse the pun!

Denver To Durango
The Colorado Trail starts just outside Denver at Waterton Canyon. Then it winds its way through Colorado ending in Durango.

The logistics of my trek on the Colorado Trail included transportation to the starting point, and again from the end; all the gear I need to live outdoors for 42 days; and food for 42 days. Needless to say, I wasn't about to carry 42 days of food (the rule of thumb for backpacking food is two pounds per person per day). The Colorado Trail is designed so that hikers can hitchhike into a town occasionally to re-stock at a grocery store before heading back to the trail.

I really didn't want to hitch into towns, so I emailed friends who had said they were keen to help me. I needed to find five people to re-supply me along the trail - another benefit of doing a trail closer to home. Actually, I found six friends! So I designated six places, about a week's walk apart. I put together six duffels holding a week's worth of food, along with a map of the resupply places, and delivered a packet to each of my "resupply angels".

How do you plan food and gear for a six week backpacking trip? I am a compulsive list maker and have a standard inventory of all the things that need to go into my pack. So I started checking off things: tent, sleeping bag, ground cloth, pad etc. The Colorado Trail book, and what I had heard from other hikers, said I would be above the tree line a lot of the time, so

I figured my hammock system wasn't going to fit the bill. I asked Craig and Steve to give me a lightweight one-person tarp tent for my birthday in June. It was perfect. Thanks boys!

I had never put together six weeks of food before, so that looked like a major challenge. But once I broke it up into breakfast, lunch and dinner, it became rather manageable. Breakfast for me is a "green shake", so I ordered six weeks of the super nutritional powder; along with a cup of tea that would get me going in the morning. Lunches consisted of jerky, dried fruit, and nuts – simple enough. For dinners, I ordered big cans of dehydrated meals: pepper steak, beef stew, chicken stew, chicken-a-la-king, beef stroganoff, and chicken noodles. I asked each resupply person to bring me a fresh salad and a piece of chicken, so I also had those "freshies" to look forward to once a week.

Since I had been in New Zealand when I made the decision to do the Colorado Trail, I stocked up on my favorite Kiwi backpacking foods. New Zealand does backpacking foods really well. I love their jerky (Canterbury Biltong – a recipe from South Africa); they make the BEST powdered milk that I have tasted anywhere in the world; plus they have great nutrition bars (1 Square Meal), and dehydrated vegetables. I put lots of these food items in my pack when I came home. The customs officers never failed to get a charge out of me!

My friends, Tom and Karen, who had offered to do my last resupply, said they wanted to go to Durango anyway and spend a couple of days. "How about we drive your truck to Durango so that you will have it at the end of your hike?" Give these guys wings and call them angels!

Once I had all my gear together, and my resupplies delivered, it was time to leave Crested Butte. I had to put together a few items for my weekend in Denver helping Craig. I couldn't wear shorts and long johns to assist at a Landmark workshop! I called Craig and asked if he could take my "fancy" clothes back to California with him and then mail them to Steve. That way, when I got to Steve's after completing the trail, I would have some nice clothes there. Perfect!

With all my gear, including my first week of food, I set off for Denver. I met up with Craig at the airport and we rented a car for the weekend. This gave us transportation and a way back to the airport for him. I love it when things work so smoothly!

My niece, Heather, and her husband, Grady, were in Denver that weekend and they wanted to hike the first few miles of the trail with me. So, after Craig's workshop, I met up with them, and we spent one night in their RV. They broke with their tradition of sleeping late, and I was able to roust them up and get to the trail at 6:00am! Heather and Grady walked the first eight miles with me. They laughed about having walked eight miles before they usually would have gotten out of bed! They had those eight miles to walk back to the trailhead, and I walked on toward Durango.

I came to a flat spot to have lunch, and propped my feet up on a tree to rest. While I was "upside down", another thru hiker came along. Her name was Liz, and I would see her off and on for several weeks. After another eight miles, I got to the Platte River. I was ready to stop, but the signs said: "No Camping!" There were other hikers there, including Liz, and we were all trying to figure out what to do. I was definitely not going to go on up the next hill, so I found a little campsite on the other side of the river and "stealth camped". Even though I was tired, I was pretty excited about the mileage I had achieved on that first day. I knew it wouldn't happen every day though.

As I had found out in the Pyrenees, thru-hiking a long trail is about 85% mental and 15% physical. There are lots of times when you want to turn around. There are times when you want to quit. But then, there are times when you are as high as a kite. Yep, a walk on a long trail is like a wild ride on a mental roller coaster. Every day you get up, pack your gear, and hike. You eat, rest, and hike all day until you find a place to camp for the night. You cook your dinner and fall into your tent. The next day you get up and do it all again – until, after 42 days, you are "there"!

Solo thru-hiking is challenging. You don't have anyone to help you carry the gear; you don't have anyone to help with navigation (sometimes four eyes are better than just two); you don't have anyone to help with the camp chores. But on the other side of that coin: You don't have anyone going faster or slower than you; you don't have anyone doubting your choice of which way to go; you don't have anyone talking all the time! To be a solo backpacker on a long trail, you need to be pretty comfortable with yourself. When that little voice in my head started talking to me, I had to tell it to shut up, but often it was just random thoughts drifting through my brain!

After about a week on the trail, I fell into a rhythm. I would get up and gulp down my "super nutrition" drink. Ewww. With only water to mix it, it tasted pretty terrible! Then, while water heated on my little alcohol stove, I would pack up my sleeping bag, tent, ground cloth, and the rest of my gear. By that time my water was hot, and I could drink a nice cup of tea.

Once I was on the trail, I would do an "hour of gratitude". Mentally, I went through all my ancestors, thanking them for the opportunity to be here now. I thanked my parents, my brothers, my teachers, my camp counsellors, my children, my friends, the people who created the Colorado Trail … each day I came up with new people from my life that I could thank. After that first hour, I was pretty grateful to be alive!

I carried two iPod shuffles. One had recordings of workshops with Esther Hicks channeling Abraham; the other contained my favorite music.

Before noon, I would listen to the workshops, and after noon I would listen to music. Some days I could skip listening to my shuffles, but I tried to never skip my "hour of gratitude".

Most mornings, after tucking my stove and cooking gear in the pack, I was on the trail by about 7:30. I would hike for two hours, then stop for my first lunch. That consisted of jerky, dried fruit, and nuts. Then, after another two hours, I would stop for second lunch...exactly the same menu as the first lunch! After another two hours, I had a nutrition bar that got me through another hour or so before I found a place to camp. By having hiked seven to eight hours, I should have been able to cover at least 11.5 miles, if not more.

Choosing where to camp often depended on the lay of the land. If it looked like I was heading into steep country, I'd camp in a level spot before the terrain changed. Sometimes I'd choose the campsite by availability of water, another important factor. And sometimes I chose a campsite because I was simply tired of walking! Not one more step!

After selecting a suitable campsite, I set up my tent, put out my sleeping pad and sleeping bag, and decided on dinner. After getting the stove going, I would heat a pot of water for my "before dinner cup of tea", then a second pot of water to rehydrate my dinner, and finally, a third pot of water for an "after dinner cup of tea". Before getting into my tent, I hung my food in a tree to prevent attracting bears. After a couple of mouse encounters, I felt that I was really hanging the food to prevent mice from eating it! Then I would dive into my tent and read about two paragraphs in my book before my eyes slammed shut. The next day, I'd get up and do it all again!

The variety of a long trail comes in the different people you meet, and the changing landscape; the forest, the alpine parts, the passes you climb and then descend, the smooth trails, and the rocky bits.

Sometimes the forests are teeming with wildlife, like squirrels and wood peckers. And sometimes, the alpine tundra would take your breath away. Or was the breathlessness simply because I was climbing a steep pass?

Many parts of Colorado are experiencing insect infestations in the forests. It was pretty sad to see so many dead trees. But it was also interesting to see how different districts dealt with them. In some places, the trees were left standing. In others, they were simply cut down and left where they fell. While in other places, they were cut down and piled together. I wasn't sure if this was for removal, or to burn them during the winter when there was more moisture.

I met some fun people on the trail. Lots were thru-hikers, and some were doing segments. But we were all like-minded; we all loved the wilderness, hiking, and backpacking. I only met one person older than me, and he was doing just one segment. I also met quite a few thru-hikers, and they were all younger than me.

Most people doing a long trail end up with a "trail name". Supposedly you are not meant to choose your own trail name: someone else should "name you". Back in the early 90s, when I was working with a high-risk teenage backpacking program, one of my co-leaders nicknamed me Talie Tadpole. So when someone asked what my trail name was, I responded with "Tadpole".

On Day Four, I met up with three other hikers: Kentucky Blue, Guthook, and Squirrel. Boy, did I dig *their* trail names! I had been really dragging that day. My back was bothering me, so I was hiking pretty slowly. The trail had been going up a long six-mile meadow next to a stream. The terrain was beautiful, but I wasn't enjoying it much because of my back. I knew there was a campsite at the top of the meadow, and just before I reached it, these three other backpackers passed me.

We all stopped at a lovely spot in the trees, with lots of spaces to put tents. After claiming our sites, and organizing our gear, we convened by the campfire ring to get to know each other. They had all thru-hiked the Appalachian Trail and the Pacific Crest Trail, so I felt a little unworthy in their company. But they were fun people. Kentucky Blue wasn't feeling too great that night and ended up vomiting. We discussed her health issues and I suggested she might be suffering from altitude sickness. She had come to Colorado from Virginia - not a good mix for altitude adjustment.

Blue felt a little better the next morning and started off hiking pretty strong. I talked with them again at the next stream as we purified water. After the stream, the trail headed up a hill, and we parted ways. Later, I found out they had retreated to a dirt road where they could hitchhike out of the woods. Kentucky Blue did indeed have altitude sickness, but by heading down, she felt better. Guthook had to return to work, but they dropped Squirrel back on the trail. I bumped into her several times later in the trip, and she finished her thru-hike in time to go to Washington State and do more hiking!

At the end of my first week, I arrived at Kenosha Pass. There was an official Forest Service campground, so I dropped my pack on a picnic table, and then plopped my body down on the bench. A lady camping across the way came over and asked:

"Are you thru-hiking?"

"Yes"

"I have heard about you!"

"Me??!!"

"Yes! Aren't you 69 years old?"

It looked like my reputation had preceded me! I thought that was pretty funny. Funny turned to wonderful, when a young man who was also camping there offered to drive us to a restaurant for a burger. Yahoo!

If someone was thru hiking without stopping, I usually never saw them again after they passed me. I was one of the slowest hikers on the trail, and that didn't bother me a bit. But sometimes, they would stop in a town for re-supply and spend a night off the trail. Then they would overtake me again when they were back on the trail. It was fun to recognize "old friends" out there!

When I had a chance to talk with other hikers before they disappeared up the trail, I said to them, "Wait! Before you go, you need the 'Tadpole Blessing'." When they asked what that was, I said:

"I wish you blue skies!
I wish you level campsites!
And I wish you to be doing this when you are 69!"

I always got a smile out of them with that, and then I felt like my hair was blown back as they were gone so fast!

After my first re-supply at Kenosha, and a newly-heavy pack, I had to cross Highway 285. That was one of the scariest moments of the whole summer! While waiting to cross, I met two other ladies who were doing a day hike. After we survived the road crossing, we started talking, and I found out that one of them had lived in Crested Butte. We had lots of mutual friends. What was that I had said in France about it being a small world?? It seems that it's a small world all over the world!

This was one of several places along the trail that was accessible by vehicles. In other words, we were walking next to or on a dirt road. For the first two days after Kenosha, I was surrounded by ATVs, motorbikes, and campers, many of whom were doing target practice in the woods. Very different from the days of walking through uncrowded wilderness areas where I only met foot traffic.

On Day Eight, the trail took me to the road between Frisco and Breckenridge. I had read in the Colorado Trail book about the possibility of "slack packing" at this point. The deal with slack packing is: you take the free bus to town and book a motel room for two nights in Frisco or Breckenridge (I chose Frisco) and spend the night. The next day, you pack a day pack and take the bus back to the trail head. From there, you have a 12.8 miles (3,674' elevation gain) hike to get to Copper Mountain. In Copper, the free bus takes you back to Frisco for another night in a bed. Yahoo! After your second night, you pack up everything, take the free bus back to the trailhead at Copper Mountain, and continue on. I was all over slack packing that section! That day between Frisco and Copper Mountain was a pretty stormy day, complete with hail, wind and rain, so I was happy I didn't have my full pack.

It was scary when a large storm came through while I was high in the mountains. Several times along the trail, I would crawl into some willow bushes and pull my lightweight tarp over me and my pack. Then it would be a waiting game until the storm cell went over. Usually, I was only hunkered down for about 20 or 30 minutes. I think it was a bit safer than standing up and hiking during the worst part of the storm...at least I "felt" safer!

On Day 12, I had my first full day of rain. In Colorado, this prolonged rain is unusual. We usually have thunderstorms that come and go. But this was definitely a "slog day". My rain gear still consisted of a windbreaker (also waterproof) jacket, and a homemade poncho that covered me and my pack.

Day 14 was my first Zero Day. I was ahead of schedule and my second resupply was to be on Day 15. So, I set up camp next to a stream and planned on staying an extra day. I started out with a bath in the river. Burr, it was cold, but there was sun to dry in. Then I washed my clothes as best I could. They were pretty dirty since I hadn't done a wash since Frisco. I hung a cord between two trees for a clothes line, and put the clothes over the line. I didn't have any clothespins (they call them "pegs" in New Zealand) so whenever the wind blew, I had to hang them up again! Then I took a short walk down a dirt road to a Forest Service campground.

I was very disappointed to see big signs on the toilets saying "Toilets for Paying Campers Only". I think the Forest Service has lost sight of the big picture! Is their goal to make money in the campgrounds? Or, to keep the forest clean? Hello?? That's MY tax money going into their coffers.

After taking care of all these things, it was still only 11:00am. I read a little, and when it rained, I took a nap, but I was pretty bored. I resolved that there'd be no more "Zero Days" on the trail. I guess they could be fun if you were in a town – but, I wasn't!

I had six resupplies lined up for my hike – one a week. I had "freshies" to look forward to, and my dear friends often tucked in unexpected treats: fresh fruit, cobbler, cookies, etc. Before resupply, my pack was at its lightest, and after resupply my pack was at its heaviest! The standard weight for a day's food for a backpacking trip is two pounds per person per day. Doesn't seem like much until you multiply it by seven – and then it is 14 pounds. Resupply was definitely a mixed-blessing!

Day 17 was hard. I had started up a hill the night before, hoping to get part of it under my belt. But as I should have learned, climbing in the late afternoon was not a good idea. I was pretty slow even when I *wasn't* tired, and by the end of the day, when I WAS tired, I was even slower! Once again, I didn't listen to my voice of experience and headed up this climb at about 4:00pm. By 6:00pm, I found a dry campsite about halfway up, and called it quits. The next morning, I was rested and ready to finish the climb. Early on, I met up with three other "more mature" hikers and we talked all the way to the top of that hill. It sure made it go faster, and it seemed easier with someone to talk to.

At the top of the hill, we came upon a group of teenagers and their counsellor. They were from a summer camp and on the last day of a five-day backpacking trip. They were so enthusiastic. When I said I was 69 and thru-hiking for 42 days, they were amazed. And when I told them about spending winters in New Zealand, one of the girls said, "I want to be you when I grow up!" What a compliment!

A couple of days later, I knew from my map that I would be crossing Morrison Creek at mile 200. When I got to the creek, I met some other hikers going the other way. (Angels again!) I asked them to take my photo at my namesake creek. As with most people I meet, they were extremely surprised when I told them that I was doing the whole trail solo.

When I got to Harvard Lakes, my destination for the night, there were lots of camping spots. I got my tent set up, then went to one of the lakes to splash some water on myself. It was a treat to have enough water at the end of the day to do some washing. I got back to my camping spot just as a thunderstorm came roaring in out of nowhere. I dove into my tent and it hailed all around me! I was pretty concerned that the hail would rip the tent, but I was very proud that my little tarp tent was able to fend off the icy deluge. As the hail turned to rain, I discovered that I had placed my tent where "a river runs through it"! The rain water kept going under more and more of my tent, and there wasn't anything I could do about it!

The good thing about most Colorado thunderstorms is they don't last very long. Of course, when you're concerned about hail ripping up your tent, and water running into the bottom, a brief 30-minute storm seems to last forever! After the worst of the hail and heavy rain had finished, a gentle drizzle set in for the rest of the night, but I was able to mop up where things had gotten wet in the tent. All was well. Except for one little thing...or several little things.

The next morning, I found my little white snack bag hadn't made it into the "bear bag" that was hanging in the trees. Of course, the mice found that snack bag, and there was a small hole where they had chewed through it. Those pesky critters!

Thankfully, blue skies had returned. I was able to hang out most of my gear and get it reasonably dry before I left camp. Not so the tent, which got packed up wet and heavy! There were still hail stones everywhere. I knew it had been a cool night, but it was cold enough to keep the hail stones frozen for 12 hours! The trail looked white as snow from all the hail. Even though it was clear, the early morning sun was not hot enough to get things totally dry. A dry tent weighs less than two pounds – a wet tent is double that! Plus, the ground cloth and other things that were slightly wet made for extra weight in my pack...and I really don't like extra weight in my pack. Just ask that postal lady in France! My plan, when I had a wet tent, was to lay it out while I stopped for lunch. By that time, the sun was high, and drying took almost no time...even if my lunch stops often looked a bit like a yard sale!

On the afternoon of Day 18, my friend Cassi's parents, Vickie and Frosty, were going to meet me at the Avalanche trailhead and take me back to their place in Buena Vista. I had a dinner, bed, laundry and shower to look forward to. Vickie and a friend had walked the whole trail, by doing it in segments. She joined us for dinner and we had a great time exchanging stories. Frosty and Vickie also had a massage chair which made my back feel wonderful – and imagine my delight the next morning when I discovered the hot tub!

Getting back on the trail that next day, I felt like a new woman. It isn't so bad when you are backpacking to feel a bit grimy and dirty, but you sure notice the difference when you are clean, with fresh clothes. Thank you, Vickie and Frosty!

Over the next few days, the trail took me along paths that were shared with motorbikes. Except for wilderness areas, the Colorado Trail is usually just for hiking and biking. I often saw mountain bikers doing the whole trail. The data book even showed the detours for the mountain bikes when the trail went through wilderness areas. Almost always, the bikers would stop and let me pass, or let me know they were coming.

When the trail coincided with motorcycles, it was a totally different story. You could hear them coming from far away, and usually so fast that they didn't see you until the last minute. I was always sure to get off the trail before they ran me over! The tires of the motorized vehicles also tore up the trail, making it rocky and rutted. With the smell, noise, and trail destruction, it was an unpleasant experience being out there with motorbikes. I didn't realize this section of the trail was shared use, so it surprised me when I first heard them coming.

While I was in Buena Vista with Frosty and Vickie, Frosty shared a magazine article with me about a "Soldier Stone" monument at Sargent's Mesa. On Day 25, the trail took me up to Sargent's Mesa, and I kept looking to see if I could find the monument. From the photos in the magazine, I knew it was close to trees. The trees at Sargent's Mesa were really far away from the trail, but I was committed to visiting this monument. I thought I could see something way on the other side of the meadows. It was a little square reflecting the sun and I thought, "That could be the monument. Or...it could be a tree stump!" But that was my destination, so I left my pack at the trail, making sure my solar charger was aimed towards the sun!

The meadow between the trees and the trail hid three swampy bits. It was rather like trying to hike across the Alaska tundra: no level place to put your foot and walking from grassy clump to grassy clump. In between the clumps, it was wet and muddy. That wasn't going to stop me! As I got closer to the trees, I could clearly see the small reflective square was actually man made. The description on the web says:

"The path to Soldierstone – thousands of pounds of engraved granite hidden in a stand of trees near the Continental Divide – is a straight 100-foot shot from a secluded dirt parking lot. From the nearby Colorado Trail, it's two–fifths of a mile. And yet until 2014, few visitors to the remote part of the Rio Grande National Forest were aware of it."

What a stirring monument. There are engravings for Vietnam, Laos, Afghanistan, denoting Courage, Bravery, and more. It is surrounded by a handmade rock wall, and I felt honored to be there.

My brothers, both of whom have passed on, were involved in the Vietnam War. Langdon was in the Navy, and was on a ship in the Tonkin Bay. Craig was a pilot in the Air Force. He was pretty fed up with the way he perceived the war was going, and signed up for a program called "The Steve Canyon Program". Through this program he ended up flying in the secret war in Laos. They took away his dog tags and uniform, and he knew if he was shot down and captured that our government would deny he was working for them. Of course, Craig loved it. The pilots in Laos were called "Ravens" and Christopher Robbins wrote a book called "The Ravens – The True Story of a Secret War".

Being at the Soldierstone Monument was an emotional time for me. There was an ammo can with notebooks in it, so I wrote a paragraph about being there while hiking the Colorado Trail and "spending time" with my brothers.

Outside the rock wall, there were random marble pieces laying in the grass with foreign proverbs inscribed on them. I thought it was an interesting aspect of the monument. If you want to find out more, there is a fascinating write up and YouTube clip at:

http://hiddencolorado.kunc.org/soldierstone/

After an hour at the monument, I hiked back through the swamps and picked up my pack. When I stopped for lunch, I lay in the warm sun and took a nap. However, just sitting around wouldn't "get me there" – and once again I was off on the trail. By now, Day 25, I was over halfway and feeling pretty strong. I guess when you are 69, "pretty strong" is a relative term! I was still really slow when I was going uphill, but I could be happy that I had made it as far as I had and was on the second half of the trail.

The next day, the trail took me down to Highway 114, and I would be resupplied where the trail crossed the road. I had been able to text my re-suppliers, Woody and Marnie, and tell them I was a day early, so I knew they were all lined up to meet me.

As I was coming down a dirt road before Highway 114, I saw a truck coming the other way. It was a rancher and his wife looking for their cows. They were towing a trailer carrying an ATV and a horse. When they stopped and asked how far I was going, I told them I was doing the whole Colorado Trail, from Denver to Durango. When they found out I was 69, they said they were impressed!

After crossing Highway 114, I looked for a decent campsite where I could see the resupply spot. I had to move multiple "cow pies" in order to clear space for my tent but I did find a level spot, and it was far enough from the road to enjoy some quiet.

When I hiked back down to the stream for water, I saw the rancher on his horse pushing some of his cows. Since there had been so many "cow pies" where I was camped, I went over and asked if he was going to leave the cows in that area. He said he was pushing them to the next meadow and I would be fine where I was.

A little while later, as I was thinking about cooking dinner, I noticed the truck had come back to the parking lot. Next thing I knew, the rancher was walking up to my tent and asking if I would be interested in a shower, dinner and bed at their place. It didn't take me a second to think about it and say, "Yes! Please!" Shane (we exchanged names now that I was going home with him!) said he was going to invite me while he was on his horse earlier, but he thought he'd check with his wife, Janet, first.

Shane helped me pack up my camp and we carried my gear back to the truck. As we drove down the road, the skies opened and it started storming. I was sure thankful that I was in a dry and warm truck, heading for a dry and warm house!

Shane and Janet were caretakers on a ranch just the other side of Cochetopa Dome. They let me do a load of laundry, hung out my tent to dry, fixed me a lovely dinner, and set me up in their guest room. I loved the generosity of total strangers along this trail. It gave me a renewed sense of community among humans. We exchanged email addresses and they asked me to let them know when I had finished the trail.

The next morning, after a delicious pancake breakfast, Shane and Janet drove me back to where the Colorado Trail crosses Highway114. While Shane took off looking for the rest of their cattle, Janet and I sat in the truck and waited for my re-suppliers, Marnie and Woody. Just as they showed up, Shane got back and he and Janet headed off to check another drainage. I sure hope they found their cows!

I filled up my pack with the new supplies, then Marnie and Woody, and their dog, Cedar, joined me for an hour as we headed up the trail. Cedar and I are old friends because she is one of my "dog sitting" clients!

Later I heard from people on the trail, that Woody and Marnie had given them a ride back into Gunnison to do their resupplies. I have the nicest friends!

As I was hiking along, I met up with a couple of other thru hikers, Wolf and Griggs. Wolf was skipping along with an ultra-light pack, but poor Griggs looked like he had a heavy load. Since I had just come from resupply, I had chicken, salad and muffins in my pack, and that was extra weight for sure. So I invited Wolf and Griggs to join me for lunch and I shared my freshies with them. They were pretty excited, and I was happy to lighten my load.

The next couple of days were tough going. I was above the tree line, so it was certainly beautiful, but there were lots of passes to go over. Finally, I came over the ridge of San Luis Peak (one of Colorado's 14ers), and reached San Luis Pass. I'd had a long day and was dog tired, so I found a place in the willows to make camp. It took me about an hour wandering around before I found water, and it was pretty rainy that night – fair to say this wasn't my favorite ever campsite.

The next morning it was still drizzling and cloudy, so as I climbed up the ridge, all the views were hidden behind the clouds. I was pretty bummed to be climbing, all the while knowing that it must be spectacular somewhere back there. If only I could see it! Luckily, it started clearing up and turned out to be a fantastic day.

Day 31, and I had camped in a parking lot near Spring Creek Pass where my next resupply would take place. Tom (my resupplier) showed up at 7:00am for an early resupply because he was going to climb one of the peaks in the area. It had rained in the night and I packed the tent up wet again. Heavy! Some girls at the trailhead said there was a yurt eight miles up the trail. That sounded good, and a short day wouldn't hurt me. Sure enough, I found the yurt and was able to go to a stream and wash my clothes, and me. The water was murky and I think the clothes were actually dirtier than before I washed them, but at least they smelled cleaner!

A fellow thru-hiker, Gumpsee, joined me in the yurt. What a cool trail name! He had injured his ankle the day before and wanted to spend some time resting it. Then Rummy and Eric joined us. I discovered that Rummy had also hitched a ride with Woody and Marnie to resupply in Gunnison. We all had bunks to sleep on and when it stormed outside, we were grateful to be in this dry yurt.

Two days later, Day 33, was probably my favorite day on the trail. I was above the tree line the whole day. I stopped on top of Cuba Pass and finished drying my tent after a couple of wet nights. Drying done, I crossed Stony Pass Road, and back into the Weminuche Wilderness. I set up camp next to a high mountain lake and watched the sunset. This was my best campsite of the whole trail! The next morning, I was still in my sleeping bag when I zipped down one of the tent doors to see the sun come over the mountains. On the other side of the lake, three buck deer were grazing. It was another of those "I could stay here forever..." moments!

The next couple of days were really good too. I'll say it again; I do love being above the tree line! The views were awesome, and the wildflowers incredible. It had been a relatively wet spring and summer in Colorado, and I was reaping the benefits. As the trail left the high country, it went down what the book described as "impressive switchbacks" – and they were certainly impressive. To add to this wonderful picture, the flowers along these switchbacks were some of the most beautiful of the entire summer. I probably took 100 photos going down this mile!

At the bottom, I met two ladies heading up the switchbacks. They were celebrating their 30-year friendship with a five-day hike through the wilderness. One of their daughters had given them little presents to open each day, and they were sporting lovely costume jewelry for that day!

They were fun to talk to and we laughed a lot before heading off in our different directions.

By Day 35, I was headed up to Molas Pass, and my last resupply. I was a little short on food, because the timing for this resupply was actually eight days. I had fixed half of my dehydrated meal the night before, and knew I could have the remaining half that night. As I came up toward the pass, I saw a little hand-written sign. It pointed off on another trail and said "Campground and …. STORE!   But the best part of this place, was the sign on the store building that said: "SHOWERS"! I thought I had died and gone to heaven!

This was the first store I had been to since Frisco on Day Nine. I bought a can of Pringles and ate the whole thing right there in the store! When the lady said the showers cost $5 for four minutes, I didn't even care. I said, "I'll get three!" and I did my laundry in the shower with me!

Even though I had a heavy pack after resupply, I felt good knowing I was heading into my final week. There is a mental game we all play with backpacking. To complete a long trail, you just have to not give up! Of course, knowing it was my last week, I was thinking it would be easier, "all the way down to Durango". Not! There were still some pretty challenging ups and downs to finish this trail.

One of the challenges on this section was water. In some parts, it was 20 miles between reliable water sources. Since this summer had been a fairly wet one by Colorado standards, I'd had few problems getting water. But I was still concerned. I didn't want to carry too much water to cover a possible shortage further up the trail because it would be heavy! Even though I was the strongest I'd been all summer, extra weight was still extra weight.

As I was heading up some switchbacks on Day 39, I noticed an area full of mountain blue bells and other moisture loving plants. It was not marked on the map as a possible water spot, but I was low on water and thought I would see if I could find some. I left my pack on the trail, and headed into the greenery. It was so lush that the vegetation was above my shoulders, but I could see that someone else had walked through here too – some flowers and plants were broken off where the other person had gone. As I followed this semi-path, I came upon a huge pile of bear poop! "Oh, that's who made this trail! Yikes!" Being the middle of the day, I wasn't too concerned, and after a little more exploring, I was rewarded with some lovely spring water. "Thank you, Mr. Bear, for letting me use your path!"

During the last few days, the route followed Indian Ridge down to the end of the Colorado Trail. The trail actually ends about three or four miles from Durango. I had met a wonderful couple from Durango on the bus way back in Frisco. They had said to give them a call when I got near the end and they would pick me up at the trailhead. Sure enough, I called Gary and Cynthia, and they came to meet me as I finished the trail. They took my photo at the trailhead, and then drove me to the local pub where I claimed my free Colorado Trail Brown Ale! Cheers!

I always expect to have some lasting emotions at the end of a long trail. But what I find is that once I have actually finished a trail, my attitude is: "well, that's that." I don't have this big revelation or sense of being different ... it's just finished. Maybe I need to talk to a psychologist about that. But then again, we know I am slightly crazy anyway!

For more photos go to: http://still-going-strong.com

Farewell...For Now!

● ● ●

*I want to be thoroughly used up when I die, for the harder I
work, the more I live. I rejoice in life for its own sake. Life
is no brief candle to me; it is a sort of splendid torch which I
have got hold of for the moment, and I want to make it burn as
brightly as possible before handing it on to future generations.*

George Bernard Shaw

I HOPE YOU HAVE ENJOYED, and been inspired by, my stories. As I have chosen a very different lifestyle to the norm, please know that I love my life!

I have learned a lot about independence. If you choose that independent route, you will have many adventures. But occasionally, you will have some consequences thrown at you. They are not judgements of your rightness or wrongness, or even of your choices, but they are simply consequences of your actions. Sometimes these consequences will help you learn a little more about the preparations for future adventures. Don't let them stop you! You can look fearless to the rest of the world, even though your stomach is full of butterflies.

What lies ahead for me as I enter my 70s? I have no plans to slow down. I want to keep backpacking and traveling for as long as I can. I think the longer I backpack, the longer I will be able to backpack, if you follow my logic.

My preparations will include alternative body work: chiropractic, Rolfing, and physical therapy. It will be important to eat a healthy diet, and to exercise. But most of all, I'll keep going to the edge of the envelope - physically *and* mentally!

I leave you with my thanks for reading my stories...and my blessing:

May you have blue skies above you!
May you have level campsites below you!
And may you still be doing this when you are 70!

Acknowldegements

● ● ●

I WOULD LIKE TO THANK my 2 sons, Craig and Steve Dobbin, for their love and support. Thank you to Glen Comrie, my ghost writer, who helped make my words coherent. And thank you to my friend, Myles Rea, who kept asking me: "When are you going to write your book?" And especially thank you to all my friends, around the world, who make my life worth living! You know who you are!

Made in the USA
Middletown, DE
31 May 2019